Theology in the Architecture of Ancient Churches in Kerala

Christian Heritage Rediscovered

The Series, as the name suggests, is meant to focus on Christian Faith & Living vis-à-vis topics like Literature & Poetry, Indigenous Philosophizing, Ethical response towards Agriculture, Health & Healing, Science & Technology, Eco-feminist Theology, Sociological approach towards Human Rights, Law & Politics, Arts, History of Ideas, Ancient Civilizations, Cultural Contiguity, Religious Cosmologies & Mysticism, Footsteps of famous Theologians, World Peace & Harmony, Global Capitalism, Network Marketing, Cybertheology, Population & Demographics, Epigraphic Studies, Contextualized Education, and many others. We welcome a Mss. on any topic/s mentioned, whether they are original works, scholarly monographs, collections of conference papers, revised dissertations, or translations of historical documents. Through the Series we, the Publishers, are striving to put forward published works that may help Institutions, Academic Bodies, Researchers, Scholars and the World at large in furthering their respective knowledge and understanding on the concerned subject. We welcome your comments on our efforts and further suggestions on how we can foster the upcoming thought provoking theologically grounded books.

Christian Heritage Rediscovered - 66

Theology in the Architecture of Ancient Churches in Kerala

Re-presents the Philosophic, Art & Aesthetic Dimensions focusing Vastu Vidya in Indian Cultural Traditions

Thomas George

CWI

Christian World Imprints™

First Published in 2018 by

Christian World Imprints(TM)
Christian Publishing & Books from India
H-12 Bali Nagar, **New Delhi-110015**
info@christianworldimprints.com
www.ChristianWorldImprints.com
Phone: +91 11 25465925

ISBN 13: 978-93-5148-278-9 ISBN 10: 93-5148-278-2

Cataloging in Publication Data--DK
Courtesy: D.K. Agencies (P) Ltd. <docinfo@dkagencies.com>

George, Thomas, 1981- **author.**
Theology in the architecture of ancient churches in Kerala : re-presents the philosophic, art & aesthetic dimensions focusing vastu vidya in Indian cultural traditions / Thomas George.
pages cm. -- (Christian heritage rediscovered ; 66)
Includes bibliographical references.
ISBN 9789351482789
ISBN 9351482782

1. Church architecture--India--Kerala. 2. Syrian churches--India--Kerala. 3. Architecture, Ancient--India--Kerala. 4. Vāstu--India--Kerala. 5. Theology--India--Kerala. I. Title. II. Series: Christian heritage rediscovered ; 66.

LCC NA6007.K4G46 2018 | DDC 726.54095483 23

Printed in India

Contents

Foreword

The religious architecture reflects the re-presentation of the sacred. It envisages the spiritual and aesthetic grandeur of every community. In the traditional architecture, the sacred space is enlivened and envisioned as the re-presentation of the rhythm, symphony and vitality of the created order which manifests the relationality that reveals the depth of the cosmic power, the mystery that is incomprehensible, immutable, undefinable and unmanifest and that transcends and transpires authentic expressions of spiritual grandeur. In traditional communities and belief systems, the cosmic power is authenticated and experienced through the ordering of the space. Ordering of space is significantly important in every articulation of religious and spiritual grandeur. It exemplifies the continuum at work within the sacred mundane polarity. The otherworldly is experienced and expressed through the dimensions of time and space. The sacred is enunciated through the mundane or this-worldly articulations because they are the viable means which are tangible and congruent with the perceptible reality. The representation of the sacred, particularly through the dimensions of time and space is epitomized through the perceivable, so that the adherents of the traditions can have the sense of the *mysterium, tremendum et facinanus* nature of the sacred which they always approach with awe and wonder.

The sacred structures replicate the spiritual magnificence and aesthetic grandeur of the holy place which reflect the ontological difference and particularity that the early church enlivened. It opens up the avenue for polyphonic discourses that brings out the ontological particularities that extols and ensue the cartography of the life-world and the thought-world. This triggers off and necessitates polyphony in matters of architectural representations. The spiritual and metaphysical distinctiveness of the micro-narratives and the exemplifications of the grand narratives and the resultant epistemological and ontological arguments, specificities and narratives constitute the philosophic and theological basis for the sacred architecture. The architectural distinctiveness that enlivened in the religious setting enunciates the need for a theology of architecture.

The concept of multiplicity and the ordering of space enthral communities to authenticate their spiritual expressions and experiences, and provide avenues to reconfigure their confessional particularities and to reorder their distinctive claims. The resultant ritualistic, symbolic capital with new hermeneutical, ideological and epistemological frames gives meaning to this spiritual grandeur. This in turn demands critical engagement with the aesthetic, poetic, inter and intra connectedness within the social, cultural, religious, experiential matrix of the community. Furthermore, this inter-connectedness mandates the re-articulation and re-positioning of the aesthetic magnificence. This re-articulation allows the communities to re/enliven the re-imagination of their collective self, and life-world. This consequent re-imagination compels the communities to deepen their faith commitments and demands, to relive authentic faith praxis that epitomizes inner spiritual experiences.

Every structure is a unique re-presentation of the idea of sacred that the community envisions. They are unique in the sense that it directly delineates the ontological particularities and the cosmic and meta-cosmic dimensions of spirituality. The disposition of the structure is to be approached not simply from the functional point of view, but also from its formal articulations, engagements and disengagements that the structure mediates. Architecture is not simply a programme or mathematical installations or aesthetic mediations and artistic appropriations but something that accentuates the aesthetic particularity and the meaning system that each tradition enlivens. The inner aspirations and the exemplifications of the collective will extol the celebration of communal moments. It has an obligation to comment on and contribute to the wider dimensions, viz., aesthetic, poetic, and the public space. The structural grandeur that epitomizes the cultural, spiritual and theological dimensions represents the theo-politics of the community. And this structure engenders the vision and the articulation of its reality. The tradition, culture, history, geographical and ethnic location as well as the ideals, philosophical and theological moorings of the community where this ordering takes place are very significant in the structural articulation. In traditional societies ordering of space and the resultant architecture in its essence is the re-presentation of power, knowledge system and notions of the sacred. The sacred architecture becomes the central place of all their activities like liturgical/ritual, social, cultural, aesthetic, etc., and bestows enormous physical resources, and imposes itself on the daily life of the user or the observer as a physical fact becoming the legitimized and structuralized affirmation of the social, religious, economic and physical doctrinal assertions of the community. Furthermore, in the activity of affirmation the structures find a representational role that is unique to its constitution.

Sacred Architecture enunciates the reification of values. The reification promulgates visions and aspirations, and ascertains the realization of hopes and alleviation of fears and disappointments. This reification is not merely of program, function or conventions, but projects as a disciplining act that irrupt meaningful engagement with the world around and provides with a text that narrates the knowledge system, meaning system and thought-world. The structure functions as a written text: a text that espouses discourses which accentuate the reading, rereading and the de-reading of the text and exemplifies celebration of communitarian moments and collective social will. The structure is the embodiment of the spirituality that the community upholds and functions as an act of communication and grammering and accentuates a coherent presentation of a discourse that takes into account the cultural, geographical and ethnic distinctiveness that provides meaning to the life world and the god talk of the community.

The typology and the imagery of the sacred architecture are very significant in every religious setting because they necessarily reflect the symbolic and ritual affirmations alongside the doctrinal, metaphysical and dogmatic assertions that transcend and transform the dimensions of time and space. The imagery of a building to represent the church is a vital theological articulation and scriptural assertion in the history of the church. This exemplification, the church as the body of Christ, delineates the essential nature of Christian spirituality and constitutive of the being and the self-understanding of the church.

Fr. Thomas George in his work *Theology in the Architecture of Ancient Churches in Kerala* brings out the salient dimensions of sacred architecture especially the church architecture in Kerala. The author examines the issues such as how the aesthetic dimension is articulated in and through the church architecture in Kerala to re-present the doctrinal, dogmatic, liturgical and cultural particularities of the community and how it signifies the distinctiveness of the collective life and the spirituality of a community. Moreover, it explores how the re-presentations of the sacred in Kerala, incorporated the indigenous forms of architectures and internalized other significant architectural forms that encountered and which has made an entry through cultural assimilation and cross cultural interactions and mediations. Every community has its own ordering of space that clearly orders their notions of sacredness and the symbolic, mythic and ritualistic dimensions of collective will, cumulative traditions and the experiences, search and expressions of the sacred focus or foci. It represents and re-presents the aspirations, ideological, theological, metaphysical and spiritual significance and the particularity of the traditions. Here, we come across the cross cultural interconnectedness, acceptance, internalization, and rejection continuum that is at work in every tradition and cross cultural discourses.

Thomas George candidly argues that, even though the churches, places of worship, etc., are built with materials of this world, they are consecrated as houses which epitomize the glory of the Almighty and where God dwells with all His/Her/Its majesty and grandeur. This should involve art and spiritual grandeur with theological symbolic nuances. This Sacred architecture makes transparent the boundary between matter and mind, flesh and spirit. "Entering the religious building is a metaphor for entering into the spiritual relationship."

Space is suggestive of proclamation and response, intimacy and participation, search and experience. Thomas George eloquently brought the significance of the church architecture in Kerala that enlivens the spirituality by espousing the collective social will that engenders communitarian self-assertion. The book also explores how it constitutes and is a constitutive of the spirituality, theology, god talk, ritual and symbolic life of the community, meticulously focusing on the architectural distinctiveness and cultural synthesis that has epitomized the construction of some of the ancient churches of Kerala. As a civil engineer by profession and theologian by vocation, the author has succeeded in bringing out the spirituality and the theological component that necessitates the structural particularity of the ancient church buildings in Kerala. Furthermore, the author investigates the issues on how the different architectural styles are incorporated and synthesized in Kerala and how this structure engenders a spirituality that transcends the mundane and become the manifestation of the majesty and glory of the sacred. The author deserves an appreciation for his passionate effort and theological conviction to bring out the spirituality of church architecture in Kerala.

Rev. Dr. V. S. Varghese
Registrar
FFRRC, Kottayam

Acknowledgement

Firstly I thank God Almighty for His Grace and Mercy bestowed upon me and the great providence which helped me to complete this book successfully.

I would like to thankfully acknowledge my Professors, especially Rev. Fr. Dr. O. Thomas, Principal of the Orthodox Theological Seminary, and Rev. Fr. Dr. Shaji P. John who lead the way towards the publication of this work. I am indebted to the Registrar of the Federated Faculty for Research in Religion and Culture, Rev. Dr. V. S. Varghese, who has been a source of inspiration and has also written the foreword for this book. I would also extend my gratitude to Rev. Fr. Dr. Ninan K. George, my research guide, who helped in the betterment of this work.

A special word of thanks to the Library Staff of Orthodox Theological Seminary and Mar Thoma Theological Seminary, Kottayam and Mr. Sibichan, Office Secretary of Orthodox Theological Seminary, Kottayam and Mr. Kurian Thomas who helped me in the documentation works.

Finally, but not the least, my wife Anila, son Ahron and family members who gave their whole hearted support and prayer for my studies without which I could not have completed my work.

Preface

The Temple of Jerusalem built by King Solomon was constructed with the command of Yahweh. It was the 'Divine Plan' that led to the realization of a House for Almighty God and not by human intervention. Worship spaces or spiritual edifices should cater to the worship needs of a believing community rather than monuments of mere pomp and extravagance. Today it has become a practice among the Syrian Christians of Kerala to build churches with huge and high rise spires, bell towers and skyscraper structures. This is a mere ostentation which cannot be justified from a Christian point of view.

One of the greatest problems today that the churches in Kerala are facing, regarding Church architecture, is the lack of uniform structure and standardized design. All the Eastern, Byzantine and Western Churches have their own architectural style and design. It has become a trend among the Syrian Christians of Kerala to raise church structures according to their whims and fancies, without even taking into consideration the basic needs of a place of worship. This was the matter of primary concern for me to indulge in such a research. It is desired that this study would help, to a small extent, in the search of the roots of the ancient native church architecture which was prevalent in Kerala, especially in the Pre-Portuguese period and to engage in construction practices suitable for an indigenous church architecture. However, there are many limitations in this field of which, the lack of proper literature concerning the ancient architectural tradition of the churches in Kerala is the foremost one.

The research is based on the analysis of the various architectural traditions and principles of selected churches in Kerala. The primary source includes inspection and study of three ancient Syrian Christian Churches in Kerala. The Methodology also includes books on Church architecture in general and books in church architecture in Kerala.

This study sprouted out of my interest, debts back to my brief years as a civil engineer prior to my priestly vocation, helped me to inculcate the technical aspects and my humble theological insights in this research.

The evolution of Christian Architecture and its Theological Implications is the main content of the first chapter. The second chapter of the study involves *Vasthu Vidhya* in Indian Culture and Architectural tradition of Churches in Kerala. Sign, symbols and theological elements in the Architecture of Selected Ancient Syrian Churches in Kerala form the third chapter of the study. The study ends with a conclusion and implications put forward by the researcher.

Introduction

Religious architecture, especially church architecture, posits much importance in explaining the faith and conviction of a believing community, about the divine. In church architecture the theme of signs and symbols to communicate about the scripture and faith of church is pivotal. The impact of signs and symbols on human mind makes it indispensable in church architecture. Likewise is the architectural design of churches. Christian Churches, anywhere in the world, has got volumes to communicate. In Kerala too, we see in ancient churches, the widespread use of symbols to communicate about the divine which in turn explains many theological facts.

Historical evidences suggest that the first wave of Immigrants into Kerala came from Syria in the fourth century A.D., owing to the persecution of Christians in the Persian Empire. According to the narration of Byzantine monk Cosmos Indicoplestus, Kerala had many churches by 6th Century A.D. But the Syrians who had migrated to Kerala had brought with them some of the west Asian conventions in church architecture. Consequently, churches evolved a distinctive style of church architecture called the 3-tier gabled structure.

The Christian architecture of Kerala has got its own authenticity and uniqueness. The most striking aspect is that it is a living entity. The Indian context is always pluralistic in nature and hence pluralistic ideologies are very influential in shaping the culture and life of the community. Down the centuries, Christian architecture in Kerala was influenced by the local Hindu, Muslim,

Buddhist, Jain and Western forms of architecture. Along with this the connection of this church with the East Syrian and West Syrian Churches also brought about many elements in Church architecture of Kerala. Theology finds an important position in religious architecture especially in Church architecture. The mind-set of the people is guided by the historical, social, economic and religious background in which they live. The religious architecture of a particular community tries to fulfil the religious necessities and aspirations of the people. In India, especially in Kerala we find an indigenized form of church Architecture.

Church architecture is a very significant subject as it is a decisive factor projecting the identity and faith of a believing community. As far as the Syrian Christians or the St. Thomas Christians of Kerala is concerned, identity crisis of the ancient heritage of St. Thomas Christian is an important problem with regard to church architecture; Thomas Christians have got a blend of different traditions amalgamated together. This creates a degree of confusion among the members of the community. This has to be clearly dealt with by properly defining the ancient traditions and concerning Church architecture by means of studies on ancient churches and its architecture. So, this book is intended to study and rediscover the age old architectural tradition of church architecture in Kerala.

The evolution of Christian Architecture and its Theological Implications is the main content of the first chapter. The second chapter of the study involves *VasthuVidhya* in Indian Culture and architectural tradition of Churches in Kerala. Signs, symbols and theological elements in the architecture of selected ancient Syrian churches in Kerala form the third chapter of the study.

Chapter 1

Evolution of Christian Architecture and its Theological Implications

Architecture is the built form of ideas and Christian architecture is the built form of theology. Christian architecture as any other religious architecture had its humble origin and slow development. The construction of the sacred place of worship was normally conditioned by the need of the locality, the economic condition, the material availability, the technical knowhow, the cultural background and the foreign contacts.[1]

Rudolf Schwarz describes that the church building as, at the same time 'an instrument of worship, symbolic representation of the deepest relationships, and a sacred participation in creating the mystical body of the Lord'. As an instrument of worship, the building provides for the convenience of the worshippers, and this requires a close analysis of physical function. As a symbol, it arises

[1] Denis McNamara, "*Built Form of Theology: The Natural Sympathies of Catholicism and Classicism*" Vol. 12, Sacred Architecture Journal (2016) http://www.sacredarchitecture.org/articles/built_form_of_theology (21 Nov. 2016).

from an understanding of the liturgy; and this implies a degree of participation in something which is, essentially, done.[2]

The primary purpose of the church is to serve the sacred liturgy. The church is the home of the risen Christ, who under sacramental sign and sacred rite continues His redemptive work among us. In this sacred enclosure the glorified Christ offers expiation for sin, sanctifies, heals, and announces the good news of salvation. The church is likewise the dwelling place of God's holy people: Christ's mystical body.[3] The sacred art of the church must possess a certain symbolic character due to the invisible realities of faith of which it is the expository sign.[4]

The nature of the liturgy as an encounter is expressed not just in the words and actions of the service but the building and its decoration as well. So, in different ways, the church building is designed to express this truth. One of the great churches of the world is the *Hagia Sophia* in Constantinople, built by the emperor Justinian and consecrated in 537. The huge shallow dome crowns the edifice, with light pouring in through the windows, thus expressing the pouring out of divine light from the heavens onto the earth.[5] The dedication of the church to the Wisdom of God identified it with Christ, the incarnation of this wisdom, and so it was seen as a body, the temple of His presence, and an animated house.[6]

The church architecture of South India has got its own authenticity and uniqueness. The most striking aspect is that it is a living entity. Down the centuries, Christian architecture in India was influenced by the local Hindu, Muslim, Buddhist, Jain, Western, East Syrian and West Syrian forms of architecture, to a little extent. Theology finds an important position in religious architecture, especially in church art and church architecture. The mind-set of

---

[2] Peter Hammond, ed., *Towards a Church Architecture* (London: The Architectural Press, 1962), 64.

[3] Ibid., 255.

[4] Ibid., 256.

[5] John Binns, *An Introduction to the Christian Orthodox Churches* (Cambridge: Cambridge University Press, 2002), 57.

[6] Ibid., 57.

the people is guided by the historical, social, economic and religious background in which they live. This chapter is a humble attempt to study about the Evolution of Christian Architecture and its Theological implications.

Worship Settings in the Early Church

Although, as the Omnipresent Spirit, God may be worshipped in all places of the universe, which is His temple,[7] yet our finite, sensuous nature, and the need of united devotion, require special localities or sanctuaries consecrated to His worship (1 Kings 8:11). The first Christians, after the example of the Lord, frequented the temple at Jerusalem and the Synagogues, so long as their relation to the Mosaic economy allowed. But besides this, they assembled also, from the first, in private houses, especially for Communion and Love feast. The Church itself was founded, on the day of Pentecost, in the upper room[8] of a humble dwelling.[9]

The New Testament gives important clues, however fragmentary, about both the form and context of the worship offered by the earliest followers of Jesus. The disciples, like Jesus himself, were observant Jews, and though at first after the crucifixion they cowered behind locked doors, their subsequent visions of the risen Lord transformed their lives (John 20:19-20). After the Ascension the apostles went up 'and were continually in the Temple praising God'. The Temple of Jerusalem had been the centre of Jewish worship since the time of Solomon, then destroyed by Nebuchadnezzar in 587/586 BCE.[10]

---

[7] John 4:24.

[8] In the Bible, an upper room was a roof chamber built above the main house, usually for the purpose of leisure. The upper room is most known as the setting of the Last Supper.

[9] Philip Schaff and David S. Schaff, *History of the Christian Church*, Vol. 1 (New Delhi: Christian World Imprints, 2016), 275.

[10] Allan Doig, *Liturgy and Architecture* (London: Ashgate Publishing Limited, 2008), 5.

House Churches and *Domus Ecclesia*

Tertullian tells us that every member of the community gave what they could for the use in the acts of worship, and for some that would mean hospitality and space in their houses for meetings of the assembly, and a private domestic setting was consistently the architectural setting of the early Christian liturgies. Typically, the dining room of the house, or *triclinium,*[11] was on the top floor, where it would be well lit and catch the breeze. The last Supper itself had been celebrated in such an upper room of a house borrowed for the occasion (Matthew 26:18; Mark 14:14; Luke 22:11) and after Pentecost new Christians broke bread together in their homes. Eventually, apart, or even the whole, of a house would be given over permanently to worship.[12] Throughout the Acts of Apostles, and in the letters of Paul we observe mentions of several house churches (Acts 2:42, 46; Philemon 1:2; Colossian 4:15), which Apostle Paul had established and these were some of the earliest Christian churches in the apostolic period.

The oldest remains that are traditionally identified as house-churches are to be found in Rome, though subsequent changes and wholesale destruction have removed what would constitute archaeological proof for either a house–church or *domus ecclesiae.*[13]

The most extensive collection of early and identifiable Christian Artefacts are the paintings in the Roman Catacombs.[14] These catacombs contained small family burial chambers (*cubicula*) with painting on the walls and ceiling. This provides material evidence of early Christian art and Architecture.[15]

---

[11] A dining table with couches along three sides, used in ancient Rome.

[12] Op. cit., 3.

[13] Domus ecclessia means a house church.

[14] Catacombs are ancient burial chambers, many in number, found mainly in Rome.

[15] Margaret M. Mitchell and Frances M. Young, ed., *The Cambridge History of Christianity,* Vol. 1 (Cambridge: Cambridge University Press, 2006), 574.

Church Building in the Syrian Tradition

For the early Syrian Fathers the whole of scripture spoke of Christ and His Church: they saw the Church through the imagery of the Bible and the typological interpretation of the Old Testament. We see that the Christianity of the Fathers was essentially ecclesial, of the Church.

Man works out his salvation in the Church and with the help of her mysteries; personal faith itself received through adhesion to the Church tradition, is saving only in the setting of effective participation in her unity and life. The most important personalities of the Syrian tradition are St. Aphrahat and St. Ephraim. Their thoughts on the Church is expressed almost entirely through typology and imagery, either traditional or freely invented.[16]

Analysis of Syrian Orthodox Architectural Heritage in the Middle East

The Tur Abdin is a limestone plateau to the east of Mardin in south-eastern Turkey. Its landscape is dotted with numerous villages and monasteries dating to various time periods. According to some Syriac texts, church and monastery building activity started in the region as early as the 4th century. However, the earliest-securely dated archaeological evidence for churches can be traced to the early 6th century. Some churches from that period, especially the main churches of Deir Zafaran and Mor Gabriel monasteries, the two best-known and most-visited monasteries in the region, have remarkable architectural decoration which make them very important examples of Early Christian architecture.[17]

Not all Byzantine emperors were sympathetic to the Syrian Orthodox Church. In fact, most of the time Syrian Orthodox Christians suffered from persecution as a result of their Christological

---

[16] Geevarghese Panicker, *The Church in the Syriac Tradition* (Kottayam: St. Ephrem Ecumenical Research Institute, 2010), 15.

[17] Elif Kese Kayaalp, *Analysis of Syrian Orthodox Heritage in the Tur Abdin for Conservation and Restoration,* Turkish Cultural Foundation (2009), UK, http://www.turkishculture.org/architecture/churches-and-monasteries/analysis-of-syrian-991.htm?type=1. (22 Nov. 2016).

positions. They did not agree with the Council of Chalcedon (CE 451) which accepted that Christ had two natures inseparably united. The main evidence dating the structures to the 8th century is the architectural sculpture, the peculiar ways of using brick, and some epigraphic[18] material. The architectural sculpture of these churches presents a stylized version of the earlier classical decoration in the region. The majority of the churches with these features are hall-type churches located in the villages.[19]

Structure of the Syrian Orthodox Church Building

The church building is generally rectangular in plan with a single longitudinal nave or a nave and two side aisles. The traditional layout of a Syrian Orthodox church is: the *Madbeḥo* 'the altar' (there may be three or more altars in a large building), the bishop's chair (Cathedra), the *Beth qudsho* or 'Sanctuary' or 'holy place', the curtain, the Gospel stand - a special lectern located in front of the large curtain and the two *Gude* - two lecterns for prayers and readings chanted by two choirs in alternation (they are in the area for the choir and deacons) within the *Qestromo*, or choir one step above the nave, the *Gurno dmamoditho* or 'Baptismal font', and the *Hayklo*, or 'nave' - the standing place for the faithful. In ancient Syrian churches, a platform is situated in the middle of the nave extending from the *qestromo* which is sometimes elevated, where certain readings and chants were performed. This elevated platform is known as the bema. The long curtain, that is often decorated, separates off the sanctuary from the *qestromo*.

Theological Implication

There are reasons for the fact that Orthodox and other Christians always turn towards the east when they pray and for the fact that the altar in the Orthodox and other churches is placed at the east side. The sun rises from the east and casts its rays in the same way as Christ shines as the light of the world. He is the Son of Righteousness that

[18] A short quotation or saying at the beginning of a book or chapter, intended to suggest its theme.

[19] Ibid.

shines every day. Therefore, the east is the direction that is assigned to His worship. The song of the sun in Psalm 19:5-6 is interpreted as a song about Christ when it says: "the Sun comes forth like a bridegroom leaving His chamber.[20]

The Syrian Orthodox and other Christians follow the apostolic tradition of facing the east, both in the building of churches and in the celebration of the liturgy and in baptism. Secondly, "for the Christians of the first millennium or so, the east had a very distinctive theological and liturgical significance: facing the east in prayer embodied their lively hope for the second coming of the risen and ascended Christ in glory, to judge the living and the dead". In this we find second coming of Christ gives another reason for praying toward the east. It reflects the eschatological hope of the early Church which awaited the imminent return of the Lord with the prayer *maranatha.*[21]

Developments in Christian Architecture in the Fourth Century

Christianity got an imperial status in the Roman Empire after the Edict of Milan in 313 CE under the Patronage of Emperor Constantine. Christianity from thereon attained freedom. By that time the church was a sufficiently robust organisation for the emperor to engage it as a partner in unifying the empire. Systems of authority, patterns of belief and control of funds and property had turned the early household communities into an interlinked, empire-wide organisation that increasingly mirrored the structure of the empire itself.[22]

The period of church building properly begins with Constantine the Great.[23] The Fourth century saw in the city of Rome above forty great churches. In Constantinople the Church of the Apostles and the

---

[20] Ayub Silvanos, *The Rite of Consecration of the Church According to the Syrian Orthodox Tradition*, 2014, https://www.escholar.manchester.ac.uk/api/datastream?publicationPid= uk-ac-manscw:240762&datastreamId (21 Nov. 2016).

[21] Ibid.

[22] Margaret M. Mitchell and Frances M. Young, ed., *The Cambridge History of Christianity,* Vol. 1 (Cambridge: Cambridge University Press, 2006), 415.

[23] Philip Schaff, *History of the Christian Church,* Vol. 3 (New Delhi: Christian World Imprints, 2016), 542.

church of St. Sophia (*Hagia Sophia),* built by Constantine, excelled in magnificence and beauty.[24] Churches were dedicated either to the Holy Trinity, or to one of the three divine Persons, especially Christ, or to the Virgin Mary, or to apostles, especially Peter, Paul, and John or to distinguished martyrs and saints.[25]

Structure of Church Building in the Fourth Century

In every large church after Constantine there were three main divisions, namely the Portico, the temple proper; the holy place or the nave and the Most Holy place or the Sanctuary. This basic structure owes to the structure of the temple of Jerusalem. In the middle of the sanctuary stood the altar, with a wall behind it and an overshadowing, dome-shaped canopy, above which a cross was usually fixed.[26] The name paradise also occurs, because on one side of the wall of the portico Adam and Eve in paradise were frequently painted-probably to signify that the fallen posterity of Adam find again their lost paradise in the church of Christ. In the fourth century, Christian worship took more precise and determined forms. The liturgies of St. James, St. John Chrysostom and St. Basil the Great date back to this time.[27]

Theological Implication

Christian life is based on two essential realities. One is the redeeming sacrifice of Christ, the need to participate in this sacrifice, to partake of communion in it in order to be saved. The other essential truth is the goal and the result of this sacrifice: the transfiguration of man, and with him, of the whole visible world, resulting in peace between God and the world. This second truth is the main subject of Church symbolism: the forthcoming universal Kingdom of God.[28]

---

[24] Ibid., 543.

[25] Ibid., 544.

[26] Ibid., 555.

[27] Leonide Ouspensky, *Theology of the Icon* (New York: St. Vladimir's Seminary Press, 1978), 25-26.

[28] Leonide Ouspensky, *Theology of the Icon* (New York: St. Vladimir's Seminary Press, 1978), 25, 26.

Eusebius in one of his homily on church consecration states that:

> The building corresponds to the worship which we celebrate in it. It is the house of God, for God lives in it with the faithful, the receivers of His Spirit. It is the heavens on earth, it is already the earth of the time to come, when God will be all in all. The beauty of a church reveals, in a way, the beauty of the celestial Jerusalem which God prepares for those who love Him.[29]

According to St. Simeon of Thessalonica, symbolically, the sanctuary represents the house of God, 'the heaven of the heavens'. The sanctuary is usually in the eastern part of the building, so that the whole church faces the east. This orientation has a symbolic significance. On the one hand, the lost paradise was 'in the East'. On the other hand and more importantly, the coming of the Kingdom is often identified with the sunrise: Christ is glorified as "the orient from on high". This kingdom of God to come is often seen, particularly in the first centuries of Christianity, as "the eighth day" of creation. The coming of this "day without end", which we await and prepare for, it's rising as it were, is symbolized by the sunrise in the east.[30]

Byzantine Church Architecture

Byzantine[31] architecture has a lot in common with early Christian architecture. The style that characterized Byzantine art was almost entirely concerned with religious expression; specifically with the translation of church theology into artistic terms. The result was a sophistication of style rarely equalled in Western art. Byzantine art and architecture can only become intelligible when considered in relation to the civilization of which it is an expression.[32]

---

[29] Ibid., 26.

[30] Ibid., 30.

[31] The Byzantine Empire, historically referred to as the Eastern Roman Empire, was the continuation of the Roman Empire in the East during Late Antiquity and the Middle Ages, when its capital city was Constantinople.

[32] Gervase Mathew, *Byzantine Aesthetics* (London: Jarrold and Sons Ltd. Norwich, 1963), 4.

Byzantine architecture evolved from Roman architecture. Eventually, a style emerged incorporating Near East influences and the Greek cross plan for church design. In addition, brick replaced stone, classical order was less strictly observed, mosaics replaced carved decoration, and complex domes were erected. One of the great breakthrough in the history of Western architecture occurred when Justinian's architects invented a complex system providing for a smooth transition from a square plan of the church to a circular dome (or domes) by means of squinches[33] or pendentives.[34] The prime example of early Byzantine religious architecture is the *Hagia Sophia* in Istanbul.[35]

Eastern Christianity made it possible for the Byzantine to establish an aesthetic experience when contemplating a religious object. Since the Alexandrian school of the third century, it had become a commonplace among Christian exegetes that the literal sense of Scripture, the letters and the numbers and the words, could contain a deeper hidden meaning. These mystic meanings could only be reached through concentration on each detail of the text, and the literal meaning was to the mystical as water is to wine. This provides the approach to the Byzantine use of Symbolism in art.[36]

Using early Christian adaptations of late Roman styles, the Byzantines developed a new visual language, expressing the ritual and dogma of the united Church and state. Early on variants flourished in Alexandria and Antioch, but increasingly the imperial bureaucracy undertook the major commissions, and artists were sent out to the regions requiring them, from the metropolis. Established in Constantinople, the Byzantine style eventually spread far beyond the capital, round the Mediterranean to southern Italy, up through the Balkans and into Russia.[37]

---

[33] A squinch in architecture is a construction filling in the upper angles of a square room so as to form a base to receive an octagonal or spherical dome.

[34] A pendentive is a constructive device permitting the placing of a circular dome over a square room or an elliptical dome over a rectangular room.

[35] Ibid., 8.

[36] Ibid., 6-7.

[37] Ibid., 7.

Theological Implication

The characteristic feature of Byzantine style of architecture is the hemispherical dome, which, like the vault of heaven with its glory, spanned the centre of the Greek or the Latin cross, supported by massive columns, and by its height and its prominence ruling the other parts of the building. This dome corresponds on the one hand to the centralizing principle of the Byzantine Empire, but at the same time, and far more clearly than the flat basilicas, to that upward striving of the Christian spirit from the earth towards the height of heaven, which afterwards more plainly expressed itself in the pointed arches. The Byzantine building unfolds in the dome a figure of the vault of heaven in sublime, imposing majesty, but detracts thereby from the prominence of the altar, and leaves for it only a place of subordinate importance.[38] The noblest and most complete building of this kind is the renowned church of St. Sophia (*Hagia Sophia)* at Constantinople (Modern Istanbul-in Turkey). The Byzantine dome rests on few columns connected by arches, and, like the vault of heaven, freely spans the central space of the church in airy height, without shutting up that space by walls.[39] The church also uses images (Icons in Byzantine Orthodox churches),[40] in order to show that a church, a place of worship, is an image of the One,

---

[38] Philip Schaff, *History of the Christian Church*, Vol. 3 (New Delhi: Christian World Imprints, 2016), 555-556.

[39] Ibid., 557.

[40] The Greek word 'eikon' means image or portrait. The etymology of the word also indicates the meaning to be likely, to be credible, to be true to something or someone. Icon in the Christian Theological context is derived from the Genesis story of the creation of man: "Let us make man in Our image, after Our likeness" Gen.1:26,27.

Icons are sacred representations, on sacred vessels and garments, on walls and panels painted with colours, made in mosaics, or out of other material and the use of which is widespread in the Orthodox Christian world. They are designed to lead us from the physical to the spiritual realm. They convey the truths and values of Christianity. Icons do not lead us to idolatry as some Christians think but they deepen our understanding of divine things and they are used to edify the faithful.

Holy, Catholic and Apostolic church, that it is the real first fruits and the image of the kingdom of God to come.[41]

Church Architecture in the Medieval Period

The religious architecture of Christian churches in the middle ages featured the Latin cross plan, which takes the Roman Basilica as its primary model with subsequent developments. It consists of a nave, transepts, and the altar stands at the east end. Also, cathedrals influenced or commissioned by Emperor Justinian employed the Byzantine style of domes and a Greek cross (resembling a plus sign), centering attention on the altar at the center of the church.[42]

The cathedrals of the middle ages were the expression of religious praise and devotion and entirely the product of the church. They served the people as a Bible whose essential teachings they beheld with eye. Through the spectacle of their walls and soaring spires, their thoughts were uplifted to spiritual things. Their ample spaces, filled or dimly lit with the sunlight piercing through stained glass windows, reminded them of the glory of the life beyond, which makes itself known through varied revelations to the lonely and mysterious existence of the earth. The strong foundations and massive columns and buttresses typified the stability of God's throne and that He hath made all things through the Word of His Power.[43]

Many of Europe's medieval cathedrals are museums in their own right, housing fantastic examples of craftsmanship and works of art. Additionally, the buildings themselves are impressive. Although, architectural styles varied from place to place, building to building, there are some basic features that were fairly universal in monumental churches built in the middle ages, and the prototype for that type of building was the Roman basilica.[44]

---

[41] Leonide Ouspensky, *Theology of the Icon* (New York: St. Vladimir's Seminary Press, 1978), 31.

[42] Philip Schaff and David S.Schaff, *History of the Christian Church*, Vol. 5 (New Delhi: Christian World Imprints, 2016), 581-582.

[43] Ibid., 582.

[44] Valerie Spanswick, *Medieval Churches: Sources and Forms*, https://www.khanacademy.org/humanities/medieval-world/latin-westerneurope/romanesque1/a/medieval-churches-sources-and-forms (20 Nov. 2016).

Because this plan allowed for many people to circulate within a large, and awesome, space, the general plan became an obvious choice for early Christian buildings. The religious rituals, masses, and pilgrimages that became commonplace by the middle ages were very different from today's services, and to understand the architecture it is necessary to understand how the buildings were used and the components that made up these massive edifices.[45]

Gothic Architecture

Gothic architecture was particularly associated with cathedrals and other churches, which flourished in Europe during the high and late medieval period. Beginning in 12th century France, it was known as "the French Style" during the period. In its basic plan the Gothic church expresses very clearly the outline of medieval society and the role of the church. The building kept the people in mind, for it was a kind of Bible in stone, filled with marvellous statues, paintings, and stained glass windows that instructed the people and evoked in them the response of awe and other worldliness.[46]

St. Thomas Aquinas has said: "*ad pulchritudinem tria requiruntur*", and these three requirements of beauty are integrity, right proportion or harmony, and *claritas* (brightness, vividness). Beauty is vital to the cathedral if it were to adequately symbolize the Celestial City, and indeed beauty pointed to God who is the bestower of all created beauty and in whose beauty all beautiful things participated. As such, if the Gothic church was to be a symbol of the new creation, redeemed and ordered by Christ, then it had to have beauty, and thus, it had to have integrity, harmony and brightness. These three elements are indeed central to the form of the Gothic cathedral. Thus, it had to stand as a symbol of the beauty of both the created order, as well as the revealed order in which all creation is made new in Christ. This is clearly a tall order, but it was believed to be possible because there were certain requirements of beauty, chiefly

---

[45] Ibid.

[46] Robert E. Wunderlich, *Worship and the Arts* (Missouri: Concordia Publishing House, 1966), 52, 69.

proportion, of which the three elements mentioned above are all a kind.[47]

The Gothic cathedral, is a model of the cosmos. This Greek word, *κόσμος* meaning order, harmonious arrangement, or even ornaments, gives us an indication of how the 'medieval' saw the cathedral. The key to cosmic perfection, and thus to the perfection of the cathedral, was geometric proportion. Coming from Pythagoras' geometry which influenced Plato, the writings of St. Augustine and Boethius emphasized the harmony of the universe and the ordering of the universe according to perfect Pythagorean proportions and ratios.[48]

One of the original reasons for developing Gothic church architecture near the beginning of the medieval period was the desire to build higher vaults. The vertical dimension in Christian life and worship is two-dimensional. God's action toward man is often suggested by light streaming down from above or through stained glass windows.[49] However, it is important to note that the medieval architect's preoccupation with ordered measurements was not at the expense of structural stability. Indeed, the use of proportion, mathematical ratio and geometry aided the stability and strength of the building, so that one sees in the Gothic cathedral a marriage of beautiful form and structural function, thus giving integrity – another 'requirement of beauty – to the building. Hence Von Simson said that:

> "Architecture that is scientific and good must invariably be based on geometry; unless he obeys the laws of his discipline, the architect must surely fail. And it is taken for granted that the stability and beauty of an edifice are not distinct values, that they do not obey different laws, but that, on the contrary, both are comprehended in the perfection of geometrical forms".

---

[47] Ibid., 70.

[48] Ibid., 70.

[49] Fr. Lawrence Lew, O.P., *"The Theology and Metaphysics of the Gothic Cathedral - part 3"* (09 May, 2009): http://www.sacredarchitecture.org/articles/a_decade_of_new_classicism_the_flowering_of_t raditional_church_architecture (14 July016)

It may be that today we find the medieval 'obsession' with Pythagorean geometry and Platonic ideas of cosmic design and arrangement to be somewhat esoteric. However, one cannot argue that these buildings have stood the test of time, being both beautiful and fine structures, thus witnessing to the science, the recta ratio, right reasoning, indeed, that was the foundation of the architect's art.[50]

Theological Implication

One of the major characteristics of the Gothic cathedral is its soaring height which, compared to the Romanesque church, is flooded with light, often mediated by beautiful stained glass windows aglow with colour. However, these things are beautiful because of the way they reflect and refract light. Light is of great importance because it is linked to the central notion of vision; light enables us to perceive beauty, and even, in some sense, to see God.

As St. Thomas Acquinas says:

> "Corporeal light is necessary as regards external sight, in as much as it makes the medium actually transparent, and susceptible of colour". The Angelic Doctor[51] also says that, "The created light is necessary to see the essence of God, not in order to make the essence of God intelligible, which is of itself intelligible, but in order to enable the intellect to understand" and again, "This light is required to see the divine essence, not as a similitude in which God is seen, but as a perfection of the intellect, strengthening it to see God".

Indeed, Blessed Dionysius, the Areopagite held that God himself was "an incomprehensible and inaccessible light" and that all creation is an act of divine illumination, so that all things participated in God's light, and there was a hierarchy of perfection

---

[50] Ibid.

[51] The title "Angelic Doctor" ("Doctor angelicus") was attributed to St. Thomas Acquinas and the reason was that he wrote voluminously and magnificently about angels. Two entire works were about them, "On Spiritual Creatures" and "On Separate Substances." In "On the Power of God" and the "Summa of Theology," he articulated the hierarchies, ministry, and speech of angels. He also wrote extensively on fallen angels in his other work, "On Evil."

according to the illumination of the thing. Moreover, it seems that light was likened with being, so that for the Areopagite, "if light ceased to shine, all being would vanish into nothingness". As such, light – who is God – was necessary for the order of the universe, and for its being.[52]

Consequently, people like Abbot Suger believed that created light was the best created symbol by which to see and know God, and so he proclaimed: "Bright is the noble edifice that is pervaded by the new light". The lux nova is both Christ and the physical light that filled his new church, and its brightness is a reference to *claritas*, and so, to its beauty. Therefore, Von Simson says that "Light and luminous objects, no less than musical consonance, conveyed an insight into the perfection of the cosmos, and a divination of the Creator." Given such a metaphysics of light, it is no wonder that the Gothic age developed an aesthetics of light that is most beautifully expressed in the Gothic cathedral, for it is by the latter that we come to experience the former. Or as Von Simson put it, "corporeal light was an 'analogy' to the divine light". Light is thus a vital element in the Gothic worldview and vision, and it is characteristic of the symbol that is the Gothic cathedral.[53]

Renaissance Architecture

The Renaissance brought a return of classical influence and a new emphasis on rational clarity. Renaissance architecture represents a conscious revival of Roman Architecture with its symmetry, mathematical proportions, and geometric order. This period witnessed the rediscovery of the ancient works of the classical Greeks and Romans. Instead of thinking of himself as a pilgrim in life, travelling through dubious and possibly even dangerous surroundings rated far more and closer attention. It is during the Renaissance that we have the beginnings of art works specifically designed for worship in the Lutheran church. In this period the treatment of Christ in the

[52] Ibid.

[53] Ibid.

visual arts shows a definite interest in His tangible humanity, where earlier art had stressed His remote deity.[54]

Theology of Renaissance Architecture

According to Richard Kieckhefer, in many places the exterior height of a church has lost its religious significance; it is on the interior that an expansive church can retain religious meaning, because the meaning of the space is moulded by its liturgical use. When a voluminous interior resonates with richly celebrating liturgy, the experience of worship comes from the interaction of the space and its use. This kind of architecture conveys a theology of profound finitude of fallen and helpless humanity bound to the earth.[55]

Baroque Architecture[56]

Evolving from the renaissance style, the baroque style was most notably experienced in religious art and architecture. Most architectural historians regard Michelangelo's design of St. Peter's Basilica in Rome as a precursor to the Baroque style. Baroque style can be recognized by broader interior spaces (replacing long narrow naves), more playful attention to light and shadow, extensive ornamentation, large frescoes, focus on interior art, and frequently, a dramatic central exterior projection. The new ideas stressed motion, dramatic expression, and size and grandeur in contrast to the restrained classical ideas of the Renaissance.[57]

Two events stimulated the rise of the Baroque style of church architecture, the Protestant Reformation (1517-1648) and the Catholic Council of Trent (1545-1563). Many of the outward signs of the Catholic Church (liturgical art and rituals) were rejected by several Protestant sects. Catholic liturgical traditions were jettisoned not only for theological reasons but also in reaction to the morally

---

[54] Robert E. Wunderlich, *Worship and the Arts* (Missouri: Concordia Publishing House, 1966), 52, 69.

[55] Richard Kieckhefer, *Theology in Stone: Church Architecture from Byzantium to Berkeley* (Chennai: Oxford University Press, 2000), 102.

[56] Baroque originated from 'barocco' meaning a large but irregularly patterned.

[57] Robert E. Wunderlich, *Worship and the Arts* (Missouri: Concordia Publishing House, 1966), 52, 69.

questionable and lavish lifestyle of the Catholic hierarchy. Art, imagery, and rich decoration, to varying degrees, were rejected by Protestants as looking "too Catholic'. A minimalist attitude toward worship was adopted by some Protestants, centering church services almost entirely on preaching. Some mostly Protestant regions saw outbreaks of destructive iconoclasm: Catholic images defaced, pulled down or otherwise destroyed.[58]

In the Counter Reformation popes commissioned splendid churches meant to wow the faithful and communicate a sense of legitimacy, power and authority. Stunning architectural and decorative affects presented the doctrines and teachings of the Catholic Church in emotionally engaging ways which aroused a positive internal response in the faithful, much like a dramatic play does.[59]

Theological Implication

In the case of the art of the new Baroque churches it was/is hard to tell where earth leaves off and heaven begins. Architects, sculptors, stucco artists, and painters join heaven to earth in amazing feats of visual illusion. The interiors of the Baroque churches often seem to be open to the heavens. Saints, angels and clouds swirl ever upward escaping painting frames and crossing over the building's architectural divisions. There seems to be no ceiling in many Baroque churches; no division, no gulf exists between earth and heaven. In terms of design, swirling curved lines and forms predominate creating a sense of dramatic movement. Everything the Church had always held theologically got a restatement in the emotionally persuasive Baroque style.[60] The Baroque reveals a sensual delight in the physical world and is a uniquely Catholic attitude in that Catholicism understands the created world as

[58] http://www.historyofchristianart.com/files/Church_Architecture_Styles_Baroque_ed_.pdf (23 Nov. 2016).

[59] Ibid.

[60] Ibid.

essentially good and capable of acting sacramentally - predisposing the faithful to receive divine grace.[61]

Modern Era in Christian Architecture

An argument for modernism as a form of religious architecture is the purity of the meditative space and the ability to focus on the crucifix without distractions. This, of course, argues against "traditional" baroque cathedrals, which achieve ecstatic heights through vaulting, gargoyles[62] and frescoes. That said, baroque churches had large stained glass windows that might reasonably have created similar epiphanies. The modernist church goer, presumably, is interested in ecstatic spirituality, while the baroque church goer is perhaps more interested in history and relics. Arguments for or against both, are of course aesthetic in nature, meaning unwinnable.[63]

The key element of the life of the church which the architecture must express is the element of interaction- interaction between God and His people and among the people themselves- the vertical and horizontal dimensions of Christian worship. This architectural interaction must find its focus in the visual representations of the means of grace- Word and Sacraments.[64] In many contemporary churches, God's action is effectively signified by a chancel cross which hangs from the ceiling or by special overhead lighting which floods the altar area with light. The trend in contemporary church architecture is to bring the altar area more and more into the main space where the people are seated, sometimes even to the point of seating the people 'in the round.'[65]

---

[61] Ibid.

[62] Gargoyle is a carved or formed grotesque (comically or repulsively ugly or distorted) with a spout designed to convey water from a roof and away from the side of a building, thereby preventing rainwater from running down masonry walls and eroding the mortar between.

[63] Philip Schaff and David S. Schaff, *History of the Christian Church,* Vol. 5 (New Delhi: Christian World Imprints, 2016), 551.

[64] Robert E. Wunderlich, *Worship and the Arts* (Missouri: Concordia Publishing House, 1966), 69.

[65] Ibid., 69-70.

The Reformed Churches in this period, upheld an alternative system in which the Bible was the inspiration of all patterns of thought and conduct and symbols were legitimate and valuable only so far as they enabled the individual to relate himself/herself to the purpose of God therein revealed for His faithful elect.[66] The philosophical basis for Modernist architecture can be discovered, like her theological cousin, in the French Enlightenment and German rationalism. What is also of note is the parallel between the architecture of the Protestant Reformation and the iconoclastic architecture at the end of our century. In the Reformation, Catholic churches were stripped of statuary, paintings and traditional symbols. New churches were designed as "meetinghouses", as if going back to early Christianity when believers met in each other's' homes. Architecture, having lost its ability to signify the sacred, became seen as merely providing for the assembly's material or functional needs.[67]

Theological Implication

Modernism was particularly attracted to the auditorium and theatre types of architecture because of their scientific claims to acoustical and visual correctness, as well as the belief that the form of a building should be determined by its function. During the Reformation, destruction of altar, tabernacle and sanctuary was commonplace, and often a pulpit or baptismal font replaced the altar as a focal point. The reformation theologians sought to give importance to the Scripture only (*Sola Scriptura*[68]), discarding many of the existing traditions of the church. This is the reason why the pulpit took over the place of the altar in the church building in the modern period. The theological proscriptions against images and symbols in the Reformation were taken up by the Modernists in the 20th century,

---

[66] F. W. Dillistone, *Traditional Symbols and the Contemporary World* (London: Epworth Press, 1968), 70.

[67] Duncan Striok, *Modernist Church Architecture - Catholic Dossier, http://www.catholicliturgy.com/index.cfm/FuseAction/ArticleText/Index/65/SubIndex/116/ArticleIndex/11* (15 Oct. 2016).

[68] Sola scriptura (Latin: by Scripture alone) is a Christian theological doctrine which holds that the Christian Scriptures are the sole infallible rule of faith and practice.

becoming a minimalist aesthetic requiring austerity and the absence of images. An essential tenet of modernism at the turn of the century was the need to break with the past, in order to find a national architecture or an "architecture of our time."[69]

In accordance with Hegel's philosophy, buildings were seen as a reflection of the spirit of the particular age in which they were built, and therefore distinct from previous epochs or styles. This was confirmed by the belief in "modern man" who because of his uniqueness in history required a unique architecture, preferably scientific, progressive, and abstract.[70]

The following are the philosophical reasons of why the buildings are important to the overall church strategy in the modern period:

Worship Facilities Can Suggest a Theological Tradition-Church buildings have been traditionally designed to highlight certain aspects of the church theology. As one moves through these facilities, the important and distinct aspects of that particular congregation become apparent.[71]

Worship Facilities Can Reflect a Philosophy of Ministry-For some churches, their use of space reflects their philosophy of ministry. Worship buildings are designed to intuitively move people from one space to another, often communicating what is important to that particular church family.

Worship Facilities Can Evoke a Posture of Worship- The intricate design, religious paintings, stained glass, and worship elements evoke a sense of the transcendent.

Churches that evoke the transcendent are quite a contrast from walking into a warehouse space that has been redesigned to house a modern church. In most cases there will be no religious symbols or ornamentation in the architecture at all. Much of the worship atmosphere is created by lighting and digital media. In reality, these

---

[69] Ibid.

[70] Duncan Stroik, *"The Roots of Modernist Church Architecture", Adoremus Bulletin, Society for the Renewal of the Sacred Liturgy*- Vol. III, No. 7 (October 1997): http://www.adoremus.org/1097-Stroik.html (14 July 2016).

[71] Ed Stetzer, Trends in Church Architecture, Part 1,

http://www.christianitytoday.com/edstetzer/2016/july/trends-in-church-architecture-part-1.html (15 Oct 2016).

differences in architecture do not necessarily change ones worship, which is a matter of the heart. However, they do reflect differences in intentional use of space.[72]

Post-Modern Church Architecture

In 1975, Charles Jenks wrote The Language of Post-Modern Architecture. In this narrow field, he defined a key element of the postmodern condition: modernist simplification, minimalism and universalizing styles were reworked with more decoration. Different styles and periods were mixed quite deliberately, even ironically. Architects no longer believed in one, dominant style. They were no longer of their time, but seemed to step beyond it and see all previous styles as accessible.[73]

The postmodern person says that truth is understood in the context of one's culture and personal experience and these observations in turn dominate how the world is to be interpreted. Instead of an objective absolute truth, i.e., God's revelation, the individual observes and accepts what he considers to be true and false based upon his experiences. This means that different cultures and different individuals will interpret reality differently. The postmodern person rejects the biblical absolutes that there is an immutable God, that God is sovereign, and that the only way to salvation is through the blood sacrifice of Jesus.[74]

Postmodernism and the Emergent Church

Generally speaking, those in the Emerging Church movement are aware of the postmodern mind set and admirably seek to adapt evangelistic efforts to accommodate postmodern thinking. This sometimes means that some Emerging Churches will feature church services and emphasize relationship, community, common traditional values, while using visual methods, storytelling, and more expressive worship instead of absolute truth constructions

[72] Ed Stetzer, *Trends in Church Architecture, Part 1,* http://www.christianitytoday.com/edstetzer/2016/july/trends-in-church-architecture-part-1.html (15 Oct 2016).

[73] Kevin O'Donnell, *Postmodernism* (Oxford: Lion Publishing plc, 2003), 8-9.

[74] Ibid., 9.

derived from Scripture and delivered during preaching and teaching. Emerging Churches use paintings, slides, drawings, and candles as visual expressions. In addition, they might show videos or television clips. Today the use of Internet aides is common and is an effective tool for communication. We agree that we must reach the culture in a relevant way, a way with which they are familiar, but we must also make sure that we do not compromise the revealed word of God and we must not let the revealed truth of God's Word be subjugated to cultural or personal pressures.[75]

Postmodernism is relativism. Postmodernism is a reaction against the logical truth structures of modern thought that gave us absolute propositions about nature, time, space, mathematics, knowability, repeatability of experimentation, predictability, etc. As modernism developed the sciences, technology, and medicine, it has helped to produce a comfortable and predictable society wherein people tend to become complacent, comfortable, and predictable. But there are always people who ask questions rather than blindly follow the status quo. Post-modern architecture may be described by unapologetically diverse aesthetics where styles collide, form exists for its own sake, and new ways of viewing familiar styles and space abound.[76]

Theological Implication

The first and most important thing about church design is that it must help worshipers to become re-enchanted with the glory of God's creation. Our primary life values have been human-centred, yet survival in the Twenty First century depends on an ability to place the needs of the planet before our own. To meet this challenge, we will have to proceed from a place of love. We all care for what we love, and our love is attracted to beauty. Church design must not only be beautiful but also must draw attention to the beauty and diversity of creation.[77]

---

[75] Ibid., 10.

[76] Op cit., 9.

[77] Richard Kieckhefer, *Theology in Stone: Church Architecture from Byzantium to Berkeley* (Chennai: Oxford University Press, 2000), 102.

St. John Chrysostom expressed the first principle of church design well when he said that it is the people who make the building holy, not the other way around. Second, no one architectural style is more appropriate than another. Third, the Second Vatican Council's "Constitution on the Sacred Liturgy" calls for the active participation of the whole assembly in its ritual acts. The layout of a church can foster this engagement with well-planned illumination and acoustics, appropriate colours and materials, ritual furnishings in proper scale and with humble proportions and a seating plan that draws the assembly as close to the ritual actions as possible.[78]

Church Architecture in Kerala

The Church in Kerala has always been a central source which has preserved the continuity of faith and tradition from one generation to the next, through the mists of time. The natural building materials available for construction in Kerala are stones, timber, clay and palm leaves. Timber is the prime structural material abundantly available in many varieties in Kerala – from bamboo to teak. Perhaps the skilful choice of timber, accurate joinery, artful assembly and delicate carving of wood work for columns, walls and roof frames are the unique characteristics of Kerala architecture. Clay was used in many forms – for walling, in filling the timber floors and making bricks and tiles after pugging and tempering with admixtures. Palm leaves were used effectively for thatching the roofs and for making partition walls.[79]

Another noticeable feature of Kerala Church architecture is the preference for Laterite instead of Granite which is seen in Stone Structures across the rest of India. Granite is a strong and durable building stone; however its availability is restricted to the Northern regions of Kerala. Laterite on the other hand is the most abundant stone found as outcrops in most parts of Kerala. Soft laterite available at shallow depth can be easily cut, dressed and used as building blocks.

---

[78] Roberto Chiotti and Richard S. Vosko, "*Worship Space Today*", *Trends in Modern Church Architecture* (23 May, 2011): http://americamagazine.org/issue/777/article/worship-space-today (12 July 2016).

[79] http://www.nasrani.net/2008/01/26/the-syrian-christian-church-an-architecturaloverview (10 Aug. 2016).

It is a rare local stone which gets stronger and durable with exposure at atmospheric air. Laterite blocks may be bonded in mortars of shell lime, which has been the classic binding material used in traditional buildings. Lime mortar can be improved in strength and performance by admixtures of vegetable juices. Such enriched mortars were used for plastering or for serving as the base for mural painting and low relief work.[80]

From the limitations of the materials, a mixed mode of construction was evolved in Kerala architecture. The stone work was restricted to the plinth even in important buildings such as temples. Laterite was used for walls. The roof structure in timber was covered with palm leaf thatching for most buildings and rarely with tiles for churches. The exterior of the laterite walls were either left as such or plastered with lime mortar to serve as the base for mural painting. The sculpturing of the stone was mainly moulding in horizontal bands in the plinth portion (*adhistans*) whereas the carving of timber covered all elements – pillars, beams, ceiling, rafters and the supporting brackets.

Churches are always built to face East. The entrance to a church is from the West. There may be an entry porch *(Shala)* in front of the nave but when one is not provided, the entrance is through the large West Door. The Door is made of heavy timber and is adorned with ornamental carvings, floral brass studs, hinges and a built in lock. The absence of furniture in churches could also be an influence of Hindu Tradition. Small mats are provided for the worshippers. However today, many churches have provided furniture for the seating comforts of the worshippers.[81]

Towards the end of the nave there is sometimes a small wooden railing or low stone wall about Three feet in height which encloses a space just before the sanctuary called the *'Kestroma'* or chancel. At the south side of the chancel, there is a stone font or basin in which infants are baptised, and when not in use, covered with a cloth. There may also be smaller altars on either side of the chancel for occasional services and requiem masses.

[80] Ibid.

[81] Ibid.

The striking feature of the *'Kestroma'* is the large brass lamp hanging by brass chains from the roof. The lamp consists of a series of graded circular trays arranged in a tier suspended by chains. Each tray hold oil and along its circumference there are little niches in which wicks are arranged and lit. When the wicks in all trays are lit, the lamp presents the striking effect of a chandelier. This lamp is called a *'nilavillakku'* which means a step-lamp, from the step of lights. In some churches the lamp is not hung from the roof by chains but consists of a brass stand with one or more trays to hold the wicks. Belfries were built on one side of the nave, but in smaller churches the bell was hung in an opening in the nave gable.[82]

From the *'Kestroma'*, three or more steps lead to the sanctuary which is joined to the nave by an arch, the walls and roof of which are higher than the rest of the church building. This is the most sacred part of the church. The tower over the chancel soared higher than the roof of the nave similar to the *shikhara* over the *garbhagriha* in a Hindu temple. The sanctuary is screened off from the nave by a curtain hung on a rod running across the arch which can be drawn by cords. The curtain is in Greek called '*iconostasis*', a screen which conceals the altar from the worshippers except at those points in the liturgy when its doors are opened.[83]

The residence of the priest and the parish hall were located on one side of the church and the cemetery was on the other side. The church and the ancillary buildings were enclosed in a massive laterite wall. There is an open cross in front of the main entrance on a granite basement in the model of *balikkal,* the altar stone. These crosses have four members: the base with a socket often fixed on a huge pedestal, the huge monolithic shaft with cylinder-like projections at both ends, the arm with sockets above and below, and the capital which forms the fourth arm of the cross with a cylinder arrangement at the bottom. All these crosses rise from the lotus carved at the top of the base member termed the *Pookkallu.* Many of these crosses have exquisite carvings and sculptures esp. on the four sides of the pedestal, and in rare cases on the shaft as the Adam, Eve, and the Serpent on

---

[82] Ibid.

[83] Ibid.

the Chengannur Obelisk Cross. Like the Egyptian Obelisks the cross is a ray of the sun – Horus or Christ.[84] The church also has the flag mast, (the *dwajastambha)* in front. Like their Hindu counterparts the flag posts are often plated in Copperor Brass.[85]

In the Orthodox Syrian church at Chengannur, Peter and Paul occupy the place of *dwarapalas,* the guarding deities of a Hindu shrine. Sometimes, a gateway like the temple *gopuram* with a *kottupura* or music room on the upper storey was also provided. Wood carving and muralpaintings, the two decorative media of temples are seen to be adopted in ancient churches also.

A famous piece of wooden carving is a large panel depicting the last supper in St. Thomas church, Mulanthuruthy. The All Saints church at Udayamperur has a beam resting on wooden mouldings of heads of elephants and rhinoceros. Floral figures, angels and apostles are the usual motifs of mural paintings. This form of decoration had continued in later churches as well. In St. Sebastian's church at Kanjoor a mural even depicts the fight between British and Tipu Sultan. The Portuguese were the first to introduce European styles in the church architecture of Kerala, followed by Dutch and British. The first church of this type in India, Santo Antonio, now St. Francis, was built by the Franciscan missionaries in 1510 A.D. at Fort Kochi. It is a small unpretentious building of the medieval Spanish type. It has been raised on a plan similar to the earlier types prevalent in Kerala though in elevation it has discarded the idea of dominating tower over the chancel.[86]

The Portuguese had introduced many innovations in the Kerala churches. For the first time, the dominating tower above the altar, which was the adaptation from temple architecture was discarded. Inside the church, the stone images were not favoured owing to their association with the Hindu art, instead images of Saints made of wood were used to adorn the niches. Generally pulpits were erected and altar pieces were ornamented in an impressive manner. Ceilings and walls were painted with religious themes in the style of European

[84] Ibid.

[85] Ibid.

[86] Ibid.

masters. Pointed and rounded arches were introduced and stained glass windows were installed. The subsequent development in church architecture in the British period also saw the introduction of a new church design. In place of the rectangular Basilican plan the cross shaped plan became increasingly popular especially in places where large congregation had to be accommodated. Apart from the obvious symbolism of the cross, this plan is more suited for better visibility of the altar from all points in the church. Further, sufficient space was now available at the transepts for additional altars for services by several priests on important occasions like Christmas.

Persian Connection of Malankara Church

As quoted by M.K. Thomas, according to Andrews Thazath, the *Nazrani* (Thomas Christians) church architecture was one with the Persian Influence. This process of Persanization existed even in the Sixteenth century. The churches, of which there are still many, were built in the same manner as 'the houses of the idols' of these parts. While considering the facts that the Persian immigrants built a church at Kollam in the ninth century and the presence of the East Syrian liturgy, it is possible that the East Syrian influence in the Art and Architecture was much older than the sixteenth century. All churches of *Nazranis* were always built toward the east, and were not mere sanctuaries when the Portuguese saw them first. In most cases, they were long-strongly built-rectangular buildings with sanctuary, nave and a porch.[87]

As in terms of the East Syrian theology, the *Nazranis* allowed no images except cross in their churches. It all leads to the conclusion that the *Nazranis* adapted the local craftsmanship for constructing sacred places along with the East Syrian usage regarding church architecture at their convenience. However, it is difficult to establish when the exact transfer took place from mere *Sreekovil*- like churches to the East Syrian format.[88]

---

[87] Meledath Kurian Thomas, *The Indian Way of Christianity* (Saarbrucken, Deüschland: LAP LAMBERT Academic Publishing, 2012), 113-114.

[88] Ibid., 115.

Summary

This chapter highlighted the different traditions of church architectural in the various parts of the world and in the different cultural and ecclesial backgrounds. The evolution of church architecture in Christendom is a very gradual process. We observe different architectural and aesthetic patterns for the building of sacred places of worship in different parts of the world; but all these edifices built for worship points out the basic fact that it represents houses of God's dwelling. The faithful who gather together in these sacred places should experience God's presence which is the primary motive of church architecture. These sacred edifices of worship lays down numerous facts and events of the Bible and puts up theological, social and cultural elements prevalent in the different Christian churches throughout the world. Even though, the church buildings in Kerala are indigenous in nature, these structures too have got a lot to communicate about 'the Divine'.

Chapter 2

Vastu Vidya in Indian Culture and Architectural Traditions of Churches in Kerala

Vastu[89] is not a religion but is a *vidya,*[90] a science. It has been developed thousands of years ago. *Vastu* only teaches us to follow the rules of nature and to balance the five elements called '*Panchbhootas*'- earth, fire, water, sky and space and paving a way for enlightenment, happiness and prosperity, from which we all, this universe is made up of. The system of *Vastu* is an admixture of science, astronomy of astrology; it is covered with the influence of the sun, moonlight and heat, the earth's atmosphere, wind direction, magnetic field and gravitation force on human beings. It gives practical guidelines on site selection, its contouring level, orientation of the building in relation to climatology and micro weather, arrangements of areas/rooms in

---

89 *Vastu shastra (vāstu śāstra)* is a traditional Hindu system of architecture which literally translates to "scienceof architecture." These are texts found on the Indian subcontinent that describe principles of design, layout, measurements, ground preparation, space arrangement and spatial geometry.

90 *Vidyā or Vidhya* means "correct knowledge" or "clarity" in several South Asian languages such as Sanskrit, Pali & Sinhala

relation to the different activities of the proposed building. Their proportions as well as rituals for successive stages of house building.[91]

The *Vastu* science is founded upon the laws of nature. The equilibrium we observe in the nature is easily perceivable by us in all moving bodies, but unfortunately we are unable to note this equilibrium in static bodies. The basic source of energy of the whole world is stored at North and South Pole. It flows uninterruptedly from North Pole to South Pole in the form of magnetic waves. Therefore, Southward portion of every building should be higher than the northward portion so that there may not be any hindrance to the flow of magnetic waves.[92]

The East is the region from where the sun rises every day of or lives, and therefore represents the quintessence of all beginnings, of all that is young and strong, beautiful, whole, fresh, full of hope and promise. The west means decline, the end of the journey, of life, of hope, of activity, but also the end of worldly attachment, of joyful and painful bonds. It faces night, the darkness of the great Unknown, beyond which perchance a new day, a resurrection may be awaiting. At any rate it is the region of rest, of retrospect and peace.[93]

In India, the south is the region of death, whereas the north represents the region of the Divine, of immortality. The Polestar,[94] which never moves from its place is the fixed centre around which our stellar world is revolving. In India, the pole star (*dhruva*) has acquired symbol-value for everything stable, fixed, immovable. The

---

[91] http://www.vaastu-shastra.com/vastu-vidya.html (27 Dec. 2016).

[92] Ibid.

[93] Alice Boner, Sadasiva Rath Sarma and Bettina Bäumer, *Vastusutra Upanishad: The Essence of Form in SacredArt* (Delhi: Motilal Banarsidass Publishers, 1996), 7.

[94] A pole star is a visible star, preferably a prominent one that is approximately aligned with the Earth's axis of rotation; that is, a star whose apparent position is close to one of the celestial poles, and which lies approximately directly overhead when viewed from the Earth's North Pole or South Pole.

equinoxial[95] and solistical[96] points mark the ever recurring phases of this eternal revolution.[97]

According to Alice Boner:

> "Sacrificial, cosmic and human elements have to be combined in order to achieve the object of sacred art: bringing man in harmony in the cosmos and with the gods and thus making him attain his goal, which is ultimately *moksa*, liberation.[98] It is impossible to escape these elemental cosmic contingencies. We are born with them, we are part of them and they live as compelling necessities in our subconscious mind. All arts are in some way or other determined in their expression by laws beyond human making. But perhaps none of the arts is so strictly bound up with earthly contingencies as are the visual art, working as they do with the grossest elements and most heavily governed by the physical laws of the cosmos."[99]

This chapter deals with the *vastu vidya* in Indian culture and with special emphasis on the principles of *vastu vidya* in the indigenous church architecture in Kerala. The following pages presents the importance and relevance of *vastu shastra* in Indian culture, sacred architecture and architecture of ancient churches in Kerala.

Vastu Principles for Sacred Space

Vastu shastra as mentioned earlier, is a science which can lend you every earthly joy if its principles are followed with utmost trust. Universe is one of the beautiful creations of nature and everything stands alive only in the limelight of truth. Just like every subject of human aspect is governed with rules, regulations and acts, similarly

---

[95] Equinox-the time or date (twice each year) at which the sun crosses the celestial equator, when day and night are of equal length (about 22 September and 20 March).

[96] Solistice-either of the two times in the year, the summer solstice and the winter solstice, when the sun reaches its highest or lowest point in the sky at noon, marked by the longest and shortest days.

[97] Ibid., 7.

[98] Ibid., 15.

[99] Ibid., 7-8.

the art of worshipping has got certain key factor principles to attain all its benefits.[100] The room for worship should be designed carefully because when you do meditation, you should gain the positive energies and then you can feel charged. If it is in wrong direction, then no matter how much meditation you do, you will not feel charged. There are certain rules which one must follow before the commencement of designing a worship room.

The *Vastusutra* Upanishad attributed to the *Paippalada Kalpa* of the *Atharvaveda* presents a challenge to various disciplines: to the indologist,[101] because it is the first text on *Śilpa* or *Vāstu* called an Upanishad; to the historian, because it reveals a situation in which image-worship had still to defend itself against the predominance of Vedic ritual, and therefore its dating and historical position is very difficult to ascertain.[102]

The *Vastu Vidya* doctrine of art-production is based on the Vedic conception of the origin and evolution of the universe from the One Supreme undivided Principle. In the beginning *Brahman* was the only Existent (*Sat*). He potentially hold in Himself the entire creation. He is without qualities (*nirguna)*, but in order to bring forth creation He assumes qualities and becomes *saguna*. The first concretization produces mind, this may be the mind-determination of the creator, but may equally be the seed of the human mind. *Brahman,* the Cosmic Creator lives in the human heart as a flame, or, as said in other texts, as the *Purusa* of the size of a thumb. He is the Life- force (*prana*) of all that exists which is expanding into the infinite forms of manifestation, yet in itself remains forever One and the same.[103]

---

[100] *Vaasthu Shastra*- an Encyclopaedia on *Vastu Shastra*, http://www.vaastu-shastra.com/worship-room-tips.html (28 Dec. 2016).

[101] Indology or South Asian studies is the academic study of the history and cultures, languages, and literature of India and as such is a subset of Asian studies.

[102] Op cit., 2.

[103] Op cit., 9-10.

Vastu Purusa

Gayathi Devi Vasudev opines that there are many stories regarding *Vastu Purusa.* As per the Hindu Mythology, in a war between *Devas*[104] and *Asuras,*[105] a demon appeared and started torturing the *Devas.* Ultimately the *Devas* pushed him down and sat over him. The demon appealed to Lord *Brahma*[106] for help. Lord Brahma named him *Vastu Purusa* and blessed him with the words: "All works on the earth will have to be commenced and concluded only after propitiating you." In essence, without *Vastu Purusa* nothing will happen on the earth. The vedas also give similar ideas to *Visvakarman* or *Vastu Purusa.*[107]

The sages have given beautiful and elaborate ideas for the construction of houses, temples, dams, towns, etc., according to *Vastu Vidya* principles so that one can be happy without any trouble in life. According to the Upanishads, *Brahma* created the world out of Five Elements, namely Air, Fire, Water, Earth and Atmosphere (*akasa*). Besides the above five, *Dhananjaya*[108] and *Sukra*[109] are responsible for the life of all living beings on the earth and their happiness. Sun, the lord of the universe, is in the middle having *Budha*[110] on his left and

---

[104] Deva - means "heavenly, divine, anything of excellence", and is also one of the terms for a deity in Hinduism. Deva is masculine, and the related feminine equivalent is devi.

[105] Asuras - are mythological lord beings in Indian texts who compete for power with the more benevolent devas (also known as suras). Asuras are described in Indian texts as powerful superhuman demigods or demons with good or bad qualities.

[106] Brahma - is the creator god in the Trimurti of Hinduism. He has four faces. Brahma is also known as Svayambhu (self-born).

[107] Gayathri Devi Vasudev, *Vastu: Astrology and Architecture* (Delhi: Motilal Banarsidas Publishers, 1995), 45.

[108]Arjuna's another name is Dhanañjaya. Dhanañjaya means "one who can conquer over riches." His brother was in need of money, and he brought money. Therefore, from that day, his name was Dhanañjaya, "one can conquer over riches."

[109] Shukra is a Sanskrit word that means "lucid, clear, bright". It also has other meanings, such as the name of an ancient sage who counseled Asuras in Vedic mythology. In medieval mythology and Hindu astrology, the term refers to the planet Venus, one of the Navagrahas.

[110] Budha - is a Sanskrit word that connotes the planet Mercury. Budha, in Puranic mythology, is also a deity. He is also known as Saumya, Rauhineya and Tunga.

Sukra on the right presiding over and dictating the course of other planets (elements).[111]

Importance of *Vastu*

The principles of *Vastu* are abundantly available in the various *Vedas, Upanishads* and the *Puranas.*[112] The modern historians Mr. James

---

[111] Gayathri Devi Vasudev, *Vastu: Astrology and Architecture*...........47-48.

[112] World's oldest literature are the Veda, a collection of religious and philosophical poems and hymns composed over several generations beginning as early as 3000 BC. The Veda was composed in Sanskrit, the intellectual language of both ancient and classical Indian civilizations .Some Vedic hymns and poems address philosophic themes, such as the henotheism that is key to much Hindu theology. Henotheism is the idea that one God takes many different forms, and that although individuals may worship several different gods and goddesses, they really revere but one Supreme Being. Four collections were made and came to be viewed as sacred in Hinduism. There are four Vedas namely the Rig veda, Sama veda, Yajur veda and the Atharva veda.

The term Upanishad ('upa' near; 'ni' down; 'sad' to sit) means sitting down near; this implies the students sitting down near their Guru to learn the big secret. In the splendid isolation of their forest abodes, the philosophers who composed the Upanishads contemplated upon the various mysteries of life and its creation – whether common, or metaphysical. The answers were however not open to all, but only for select students. The reason for this was simple: not everyone can handle knowledge. There are 18 principal Upanishads.

The Puranas are a genre of important Hindu, Jain and Buddhist religious texts, notably consisting of narratives of the history of the universe from creation to destruction, genealogies of kings, heroes, sages, and demigods, and descriptions of Hindu cosmology, philosophy, and geography. Puranas usually give prominence to a particular deity, usually written in the form of stories related by one person to another. Brahmin scholars read from them and tell their stories, usually in Katha sessions (in which a traveling Brahmin settles for a few weeks in a temple and narrates parts of a Purana).

Vastu is a part of Vedas, which are believed to be four to five thousand years old. Through penance and meditation yogis of that period acquired answers believed to have come from the cosmic mind itself to their questions. Hence, Vedas are heeded with divine knowledge. The art of Vastu originates in the Stapatya Veda, a part of the Atharva Veda.

It used to be a purely technical subject and it was only confined to architects (Sthapatis) and handed over to their heirs. The principles of construction, architecture, sculpture, etc., as enunciated in the epics and treatise on temple architecture, have been incorporated in the science of vastu. Its description is there

Ferguson, Dr. Havell and Sir Cunning Ham have come to the conclusion that the historic development of *Vastu shastra* took place during the period 6000 B.C. to 3000 B.C.[113] A dive deep into the unfathomable depths of the intellectual feat of the ancient masters into ancient manuscripts reveals beyond doubt the principles recorded are geological, geometrical, geophysical, botanical and above all cosmological and celestial. To understand the mind of the *Maharishis*[114] and how *Vastu* discipline is designed, it is necessary to know the cosmogony of the universe, the position of the earth and how the earth is being influenced by the celestial spheres.[115] All objects in Nature whether mineral, vegetable or animal are produced, protected and perish under the influence of the solar ray. The solar light is scientifically split into three segments, first, a visible spectrum of coloured rays, ranging from the deepest blue to the deepest red with different wave lengths flanked by two invisible zones known as ultra-violet and infra-red.[116]

It is worth studying the findings of Gayathri Devi Vasudev, according to which man is essentially cosmic in character. The earth is made up of cosmic materials and Nature radiates cosmic forces.[117] The interplay of cosmic forces between the objects in Nature and

in epics like Mataysya Purana, Skanda Purana, Agni Purana, Garuda Purana, and Vishnu Purana. There are some other ancient shastras that pass over the knowledge of vastu shastra to next generation, like Vishvakarma Prakash, Samraangan Sutradhar, Kashyap Shilpshastra, Vrihad Sanhita, and Praman Manjaree.

113 Gayathri Devi Vasudev, *Vastu: Astrology and Architecture*.......... 74.

114 maharishi- a great Hindu sage or spiritual leader.

115 Gayathri Devi Vasudev, *Vastu: Astrology and Architecture*.......... 75.

116 Ibid., 75.

117 Relevance of Vastu- A study of ancient literature bearing on Jyotisa, medicine, Vastu, etc., will reveal that the vision of ancient sages was far more deeply based on, and intimately correlated to the realities and values of life than dreamt of in modern times. A careful examination of Hindu methodology which is necessary for a right understanding of Hindu attainments in Vastu Shastra reveals that the whole movement was genuinely and positively scientific, the ultimate goal being spiritual; and it was arrested at an important stage due to political convulsions. An essential difference between the approach of Rishes and modern science is that the former is comprehensive, integral, holistic and spiritual; while the latter is mostly adhoc, fragmentary, reductionist and mechanistic.

man are fully reflected in the discipline and principles of *Grha-vastu,*[118] *Grama-vastu,*[119] *Pattana-vastu,*[120] *Nagara-vastu*[121] *and Raja-grha-vastu.*[122] The experience of many generations has proved that the planning of the village, towns, cities and capitals of ancient India was best and it gave health and happiness and also prosperity to the people.

Vastu principles are more or less common all over India, living from times immemorial as acultural entity. *Vastu* has retained its traditions for thousands of years and it is relevant today as it was when first propounded. *Gautamiyam, Bauddhatam and Caitya* are the Vastu texts for Jainism and Budhism. The *Vastu Silpa* traditions is purely Indian in its fundamental concepts and currency.[123] P. V. Joseph is of the opinion that, in India *Vastu Shastra* is considered as a rule for harmonious life rather than a subject of science. This is called *Vastu* because it itself is evolved from *Vastu.* Interestingly, practically none of the practitioners of *Vastu Shastra* has an academic background. So there is a lot of genuine practice as well as hearsay going around.[124] The term *vāstu* is referred to all things which is created by God and this when used for different purposes is called *vastu.*[125] *Vastu shastra* has two divisions, namely the *vastu* for painting and *vastu* for places of dwelling. In the latter there are again a division-for human dwelling and places of worship. *Kautalya*[126] in his work '*Arthasastra*', explains *vastu* as *'grha-kshetra-arama-sethubanda-thadaga-matharo-va-vastu*, which means house-temple-garden-tanks-

---

[118] Grha Vastu- vastu principles for places of dwelling.

[119] Grama Vastu- vastu principles for village layout.

[120] Pattana Vastu- vastu principles for town planning.

[121] Nagar Vastu- vastu principles for city development.

[122] Raja Grha Vastu- vastu principles for palace construction.

[123] Ibid., 5.

[124] Muktirajsinhji Chauhan, *Vastu Shastra - Sacred Architecture of India*, http:// archaeologyonline.net/artifacts/vastu-shastra (24 Feb. 2017).

[125] P. V. Joseph, *Keraliya Vastuvidya Paramparyam* (Kozhikode: Mathrubhumi Books, 2012), 113.

[126] *Kautalya-Chanakya* was an Indian teacher, philosopher, economist, jurist and royal advisor. He is traditionally identified as *Kauṭilya or Vishnugupta*, who authored the ancient Indian political treatise, the *Arthashastra.*

bridges-well-pond-artificial lakes, etc., and human beings, all which helps in journeying and working is understood as *vastu.*[127]

Efficacy of *Vastu*

The main objective of *vastu shastra* is to make humanity live in as perfect a harmony as possible with Mother Nature.[128] This *sastra* was given by the *maharsis.*[129] The area is divided into eight parts: East, South, West, North, North-East, South-East, South-West and North-West. Each of these directions has a deity called *Dikpāla.*[130] The *Dikpālas* are as follows:

East	Indra	South-East - *Agni*
South	Yama	South-West - *Nirrti*
West	Varuna	North-West - *Vāyu*
North	Kubera	North-East - *Iśāna*

The vedic texts have given different hymns to the eight *Dikpālas.* Indra is the king of the *Devatas.* The sun rises on the eastern horizon. Hence, east is given the most prominent place followed by North, the direction of *Kubera,* the lord of wealth. East is the point of health, virtuous living, and fame. North is the point of wealth, name, prosperity. North has astronomical significance also as it points towards the Pole-star[131] or the *Dhruva Nakshatra.*[132]

---

[127] Gayathri Devi Vasudev, *Vastu: Astrology and Architecture*................. 113..

[128] Ibid., 141.

[129] Maharshi- a Hindu sage or sanyasin.

[130] Gayathri Devi Vasudev, *Vastu: Astrology and Architecture*..............141.

[131] Ibid., 114.

[132] Dhruva is a devotee of the Supreme God Vishnu according to Hinduism. Dhruva was the son of Uttānapāda. His tale is recorded in the Vishnu Purana and the Bhagavata Purana.

North Pole Star is called Dhruva Nakshatra in Sanskrit literature. This identification is said to be coming from Dhruva. This is because of the boon he receives from Brahma. The other interpretation is, Dhruv was immovable in his resoluteness of meditation. In the sky, the pole star (polaris) is noted for its fixed

Vastu: A Result Oriented Science

In the present day of urbanisation and sophisticated modernisation, the principles of *vastu-shastra* are still applicable. The effects, good or bad, which have been ascribed to particular directions are still found to work. In the construction of house, apartment, or a building, the well-being of the occupants from every angle is of prime importance in *vastu-shastra.* Orientation of any premises considering the cardinal principles of every direction is an essential part while planning the constructions.[133] In the Vedic period, the Rishis and their *asramas*[134] and *parnakutis*[135] on the bank of rivers, and those were placed in such a way that no time would there be any imbalance between Nature and the *asrama;* all the rules of *vastu-shastra* were followed.[136]

Vastu and Hindu Temple Architecture

Hindu temples became popular in the 6th C.E. All the temples of this period has one feature in common. The *girbha grha* is a room without any lighting. In front of the *girbha grha* is the *mandapa*[137] for worship. The roof of the *girbha grha* was constructed in the form of a stupa[138] in order to exhibit the importance of the *girbha grha.*[139] Scientifically this is called *vimana.*[140]

---

position. It is possible that Dhruv was renamed for his resoluteness after the pole star.

[133] Gayathri Devi Vasudev, *Vastu: Astrology and Architecture*.........146.

[134] Asrama- Traditionally, an ashram (or ashramam) is a spiritual hermitage or a monastery in Indian religions.

[135] Parnakuti- A hut of leaves and grass; applied modestly or contemptuously to a dwelling house.

[136] Ibid., 147.

[137] Mandapa- in Indian architecture is a pillared outdoor hall or pavilion for public rituals.

[138] A stupa is a mound-like or hemispherical structure containing relics that is used as a place of meditation.

[139] Girbhagriha or Garbhagruha is the sanctum sanctorum, the innermost sanctum of a Hindu temple where resides the murti of the primary deity of the temple.

[140] Vimana is a term for the tower above the Garbhagriha or Sanctum sanctorum in a Hindu temple.

The South-Indian vastu pattern has got many sub-divisions, namely the *Chola,*[141] *Pandya,*[142] *Chalukya,*[143] *Pallava,*[144] *Hoisala,*[145] *Vijayanagara,*[146] etc. These patterns were rampant in South India during the 6th and 18th century C.E.[147]

Vastu and Buddhist Architecture

The size of Buddhism's contribution to the world of architecture is enormous. There are two basic types of structure found in those places where Buddhism spread and developed and they are the *Vihara*[148] and the Stupa.[149] One of the most famous cave complexes is the magnificently embellished caves at Ajanta, with its brightly coloured Buddhist murals. The earliest examples of Buddhist stupa were raised in India, the dome shaped stupa at Sanchi, the ancient

---

[141] The Chola dynasty was one of the longest-ruling dynasties in the history of southern India. The earliest datable references to this Tamil dynasty are in inscriptions from the 3rd century BCE left by Ashoka, of the Maurya Empire.

[142] The Pandyan or Pandiyan or Pandian dynasty was an ancient Tamil dynasty, one of the three Tamil dynasties, the other two being the Chola and the Chera.

[143] The Chalukya dynasty was an Indian royal dynasty that ruled large parts of southern and central India between the 6th and the 12th centuries. During this period, they ruled as three related yet individual dynasties.

[144] The Pallava dynasty was a South Indian dynasty that existed from 275 CE to 897 CE, ruling a portion of what is today southern India. They gained prominence after the eclipse of the Satavahana dynasty, whom the Pallavas served as feudatories. Pallavas became a major power during the reign of Mahendravarman I (571 – 630 CE) and Narasimhavarman I (630 – 668 CE) and dominated the Telugu and northern parts of the Tamil region for about 600 years until the end of the 9th century.

[145] The Hoysala empire was a prominent Southern Indian Kannadiga empire that ruled most of the modern-day state of Karnataka between the 10th and the 14th centuries.

[146] The Vijayanagara Empire (also called Karnata Empire, and the Kingdom of Bisnegar by the Portuguese) was based in the Deccan Plateau region in South India.

[147] Mohanakshan Nair A., *Vasthuvidya Christhava-Muslim Devalayangal* (Kottayam: D C Press (P) Ltd., 2009), 72.

[148] Vihara-means 'an abode'; its function was two-fold. It was inented to house Buddha images and art and also to serve as a dwelling place for monks.

[149] Stupa-is an object of worsip as it was intented to serve as arelic chamber for the Buddha's remains.

Dhamekh Stupa at Sarnath and those built inside the caves at Ellora and Ajanta.[150] *Chaitya grihas*[151] or halls of worship were built all over India either of brick or excavated from rocks. Ruins of a large number of structural Buddhist *chaitya grihas* are found in the eastern districts of Andhra Pradesh, in valleys, near rivers and lakes.[152] The *chaitya* has a double-storeyed façade and has three doorways in the lower part. It has an upper gallery over which there is an arch. The walls of the vestibule to the *chaitya* hall are decorated with sculptured figures. The pillars separating the central nave from the aisles have a pot base, an octagonal shaft, and inverted lotus capital[153] with an abacus. The *chaitya*s have a vaulted ceiling with a huge horse-shoe shaped window over the doorway. They are large halls divided into three parts, the central nave, apse and aisles on either side separated by a row of columns.[154]

Vastu and Jain Architecture

From the first century onwards Mathura[155] became the centre of Jain artistic activities. Of the Jain caves of the post-Gupta period reference may be made to one at Badami and another at Aihole, both assignable to the middle of seventh century AD. The best known Jain cave temple is the *Indra Sabha* which is cut out of solid rock. In the centre of the court there is a square *mandapa* and beyond it the

---

[150] Suraj Vashishth, *A Handbook of Buddhism: Art, Architecture, Literature and Philosophy* (New Delhi: Cyber Tech Publications, 2009), 10.

[151]A chaitya is a Buddhist shrine or prayer hall with a stupa at one end. In modern texts on Indian architecture, the term chaitya-griha is often used to denote an assembly or prayer hall that houses a stupa.

[152] Mohanakshan Nair A., *Vasthuvidya Christhava-Muslim Devalayangal*...... 19.

[153] In architecture the capital (from the Latin caput, or "head") or chapiter forms the topmost member of a column (or a pilaster). It mediates between the column and the load thrusting down upon it, broadening the area of the column's supporting surface. The capital, projecting on each side as it rises to support the abacus, joins the usually square abacus and the usually circular shaft of the column.

[154] Mohanakshan Nair A., *Vasthuvidya Christhava-Muslim Devalayangal*...... 20.

[155] Mathura is a city in the North Indian state of Uttar Pradesh. Mathura is believed to be the birthplace of Krishna which is located at the centre of Braj or Brij-bhoomi, called Shri Krishna Janma-Bhoomi, literally: 'Lord Krishna's birthplace'.

passage there are two big images of *Santinatha,*[156] and at the right the stairway leading to the upper hall of the temple.[157]

References to *Vastu* in the Scriptures

Vastu is based on mathematical, geomagnetic, philosophical and metaphysical concepts. These concepts are no abstractions, but living forces which become operative in determining the direction of our lives. Branching out of sculpture, the science of *vastu or silpa* finds numerous references, implicit and explicit in the Vedas, *Brahmanas, Upanishads and Puranas.*[158]

Vastu is derived from the verb *'vas'* meaning 'to dwell', or place of residence. *Vastospati,* the Lord of a house, is a deity in the *Rigveda.* It also applies to conveyances, furniture and all constructed structures. The principal *vastu,* however, is the ground on which others rest.[159]

During the medieval period, vast body of Sanskrit references, independent architectural manuals were written, without reservation, and scattered across the country. Apparently, some attempts were made to classify and evaluate their contents in a systematic way. Of the many such attempts that tried to bring about order and coherence in the various theories and principles of temple construction, the most well-known compilations are *Manasara* and *Mayamata.* They are the standard texts on *Vastu Shastra,* and they codify the theoretical aspects of all types of constructions; but specifically of temple construction. These texts deal with the whole range of architectural science including topics such as soil testing techniques, orientation, measures and proportion, divination, astrology and ceremonies associated with the construction of buildings.[160]

---

[156] Shantinath is especially revered in the Jain pantheon. He is the 16th Jina (saviour-teacher) and is said to have revived Jainism at a time when it was in danger of extinction, assuring the faith's survival. Over time Jains came to invoke him to avert calamities and ensure the peace his name suggests (santi, 'peace'; natha,'lord').

[157] N. N. Bhattacharya, *Jain Philosophy: Historical Outline* (Delhi: Munshiram Manoharlal Publishers Pvt. Ltd, 1999), 48, 51.

[158] P. V. Joseph, *Keraliya Vastuvidya Paramparyam*..................... 181.

[159] Ibid., 181.

[160] Sreenivasa Rao S., *Temple Architecture-Devalaya Vastu,* https://sreenivasaraos.com/2012/09/07/temple-architecture-devalaya-vastu-part-one-1-of-7 (24 Jan. 2017).

Manasara is a comprehensive treaty on architecture and iconography. It represents the universality of *Vastu* tradition and includes the iconography of Jain and Buddhist images. The work is treated as a source book and consulted by all. The *Mayamata* too occupies an important position. It is a general treatise on *Vastu shastra*; and is a text of Southern India. It is regarded a part of *Shaiva* literature and might belong to the *Chola* period when temple architecture reached its peak. It is the best known work on *Vastu.* The work is coherent and well structured. It defines *Vastu* as the arrangement of space, anywhere, wherein immortals and mortals live.[161]

These subjects are intertwined with Astrology. The *Vastu* texts believe that *Vigraha* (icon or image of the deity) is closely related to *Graha* (planets). The term *Graha* literally means that which attracts or receives; and *Vigraha* is that which transmits. It is believed that the idols receive power from the planets; and transmit the power so received. It not merely is a symbolism but also one that provides logic for placement of various deities in their respective quarters and directions.[162]

---

[161] Ibid.

[162] Ibid.

The *Vastu* of Temples

The *Agamas*[163] are the basis for Indian *Vastu* and sculpture. *Kriyapada*[164] of each *Agama* deals with temple construction and sculpture installation procedure, house construction, *vastu-puja*, specialities of *Silpa,* etc. With reference to the *Kamikagama,*[165] the temple *vastu* is classified into sixteen kinds and the *grha vastu* into forty-five kinds. Temple *vastu* is also classified into *'Nagara', 'vesara' and 'dravida.'*[166] The main object of Indian sculpture from the ancient age is to establish the relation between man and the material world. Body is temple and soul is God. To signify God's power of creating the body construction, and its survival for the

---

[163] Agamas and Tantras are a vast collection of knowledge and form a major portion of spiritual literature and practices. Like the Veda, they have come down through Guru-Sishya parampara, in oral traditions. Agamas form the base for many of the popular as well as specialist aspects of Hinduism. The word Agama means 'that which has come to (us)'. Tantra means 'that which protects with detail'. Sruti, the eternal word, is said to be of two forms – Nigama (Veda) and Agama. Two kinds of texts, Agama and Tantra are in general grouped under the same class of literature. There are three main classes of Agamic/Tantric texts Vaishnava Agamas, Saiva Agamas and Sakta Tantras, though not limited to these. The Vaishnava and Saiva texts are generally called Agamas, while the word Tantra in general applies to Sakta texts. However, technically Tantra is a part of Agama and owing to the centrality of Tantra the two words are used often interchangeably.

[164] Kriya Pada deals with the religious aspect such as temple construction, domestic and temple rituals, pilgrimage. It also gives procedures for worship, ritual codes and the ingredients of worship.

[165] Kamikagama is one of the longest Agamas followed by most of the temples in South India. It is looked up on as the feet of Siva. It deals with all the rituals from karshana (turning the sod) to pratishta (installation) of deities.

[166] Nagara architecture. Architecture of the Khajuraho temples. Nagara temples have two distinct features : In plan, the temple is a square with a number of graduated projections in the middle of each side giving a cruciform shape with a number of re-entrant angles on each side Vesara (or Karnataka Dravida or Chalukyan or Deccan style) is a type of Indian architecture primarily used in temples lying in the region between the Vindhyas and the river Krishna.

Dravidian architecture was an architectural idiom that emerged in the Southern part of the Indian subcontinent or South India. It consists primarily of temples with pyramid shaped towers and are constructed of sandstone, soapstone or granite.

devotee, through *silpa vastu,* the temples are constructed.[167] For performing the *yagnas,*[168] halls called as *vamsas,*[169] terraces and platforms were constructed with bamboo, brick and timber. They were called *vedikas.*[170] For different *yajnas,* different types of *vedikas* were available. Temples are of two kinds, viz., cave temples and constructed temples. Temples constructed by drilling the caves are called cave temples, and temples. Temple construction includes various halls in one complex, such as *girbhagrha and antarala,*[171] *mukha-mandapa, vimana,*[172] *prakara,*[173] *mahadvara,*[174] *dvaramandapa,* kitchen, resting hall, car hall, etc., with the temple complex. The construction above the base and below the building is called *adisthana* which must be strong. The *adisthana* is different for different lands of construction.[175] *Girbhagrha, mandapa,* the path

---

[167] P. V. Joseph, *Keraliya Vastuvidya Paramparyam*.................. 188.

[168] Yajna literally means "sacrifice, devotion, worship, offering", and refers in Hinduism to any ritual done in front of a sacred fire, often with mantras. Yajna has been a Vedic tradition, described in a layer of Vedic literature called Brahmanas, as well as Yajurveda. The tradition has evolved from offering oblations and libations into sacred fire to symbolic offerings in the presence of sacred fire (Agni).

Yajna rituals-related texts have been called the Karma-kanda (ritual works) portion of the Vedic literature, in contrast to Jnana-kanda (knowledge) portion contained in the Vedic Upanishads. The proper completion of Yajna-like rituals was the focus of Mimansa school of Hindu philosophy. Yajna have continued to play a central role in a Hindu's rites of passage, such as weddings. Modern major Hindu temple ceremonies, Hindu community celebrations, or monastic initiations may also include Yajna vedic rites, or alternatively be based on agamic rituals.

[169] Vaṃśa denoting the 'rafters' or 'beams' of the house as made of bamboo cane, is found in this sense from the Rigveda onwards.

[170] Vedika- is a balustrade used in Hindu temple architecture.

[171] Antarala (Sanskrit: lit. intermediate space) is a small antechamber or foyer between the garbhagriha (shrine) and the mandapa, more typical of north Indian temples.

[172] Vimana-The Sanskrit word vi-māna literally means "measuring out, traversing" or "having been measured out. It is a feature of Hindu temple architecture.

[173] A Prakaram also spelled Pragaram or Pragaaram, in Indian architecture is an outer part around the Hindu temple sanctum. These may be enclosed or open and are typically enclosed for the inner most prakaram.

[174] Maha Dwaram is the main entrance of the Temple.

[175] Op cit.., 190.

for circumambulation and surrounding walls are constructed on the *adisthana*. According to the direction of the *mula vigraha*, i.e., the image of the principal, deity, the entrance will be determined either on the eastern side or the northern side.[176]

Vastu of Temples in Kerala

According to the Stone inscriptions, there are evidences of the presence of *Kshetras*[177] or temples from the 7th Century C. E. In the 7-8th centuries there were cave temples. In this period itself, there were temples with square and circular planned *Sreekovil*[178] in Kerala. All these constructions were simple and single structured. These were small *girbha griha* for housing the *Bhimba.*[179] In due course of time to the small structures, *artha mandapas* were built as auxiliary structures. The temple at villages has *chuttambalam*[180] and is encircled by *balikallu.*[181] Along with this is the *vilakkumadam*[182] and all these exist as a single unit or building.[183]

---

[176] Op cit., 190.

[177] In Sanskirt 'Kshetram' stands for 'temple', in Malayalam it is 'Ambalam'. It is derived from Om+ Phalam= Ambalam. Ambalam can be defined as a place where the Cosmic sound 'Om'(Aum) actualizes its existence in reality.

[178] *sreekovil- girbha grha-Sree Kovil* (Sanctum Sanctorum)is the most sacred structure where the presence of God is believed.

[179] *Bimbha-* idol of the deity installed in the *sreekovil* of the temple.

[180] Generally the temple complex of Kerala falls under the *Pancha Prakara* (five enclosures around the Sanctum Sanctorum). They are (i*) Akathe Balivattom* (inner-most part), (ii) *Chuttambalam or Nalambalam* (second enclosure), (iii*) Vilakkumadam* (third enclosure), (iv) *Purathe Balivattom or Sivelippura* (place where *Bali Peetas* and subsidiary deities are installed), and (v) *Maryada or Puram Mathil* (outer wall). Each *Prakara* keepsa specified distance from the *Sree Kovil* (Sanctum sanctorum).

[181] *Balikkal* is at the front of the main entrance of the deity. The position of the *Valia Balikkal* is at the prescribed distance from the centre of the *Sree Kovil. Bali peeta* is a platform for offering to the deities.

[182] *vilakkumadam-* It is a structure with column fixed with innumerable lamps. It is located 5 or 10 feet fromthe inner side of the wall of *Nalambalam.*

[183] Mohanakshan Nair A., *Vasthuvidya Christhava-Muslim Devalayangal* (Kottayam: D C Press (P) Ltd., 2009), 72.

Indeed almost all these auxiliary structures, especially the external features that we observe in Hindu temples were present in ancient *Nazrani* churches in Kerala. It is a fact that the church of Kerala or Malankara[184] church is culturally, socially and architecturally indigenous in nature and the social and cultural life of this church bears close resemblance with that of the local people and customary.

Joseph Cheeran agrees with modern secular historian A. Sreedhara Menon saying:

Most of the Kerala temples were built in the 8th century C.E. This tradition progressed during the period of the Kulashekara emperors (800-1102). This was the period during which most of the Hindu temples in Kerala were built. By this time Christian-Islamic-Jewish religions had also built their own centres of worship and had started attracting local communities through their creeds and worship.[185]

Spatial Organisation of the Temple of Jerusalem

The Temple of Jerusalem was a place of worship, but unlike modern churches it was not designed for communal use. Its inner chamber was a focal point for the deity's presence, and entrance was prohibited to ordinary people. The First Temple was completed in 957 B.C, the Second Temple in 515 B.C, and Herod's Temple was completed in 26 A.D. Solomon completed the First Temple, the exiles returned from Babylon built the Second Temple, and Herod the Great completed a rebuilding of the Temple during the Roman era.[186]

The building of the Temple occupied Solomon from the fourth to the eleventh year of his reign.[187] He made a contract with Hiram, king of Tyre, for the timber to be brought from Lebanon, while the stone was quarried near Jerusalem.[188] The Israelites were conscripted to provide the bulk of the Labour force, but the skilled workmen were Phoenicians. The Temple was a long building, open on one of

[184] Malankara church is the church of the St. Thomas Christians of Kerala.

[185] Op cit., 30.

[186] http://www.bible-architecture.info/Jerusalem.htm (28 Jan. 2017).

[187] 1 Kings 6:37-38; cf 6:1.

[188] I Kings 5:19, 31.

its shorter sides. The interior was divided into three parts: vestibule, called the *Ulam* (from a root meaning 'to be in front of'), a room for worship called the *Hekal* (which has the double meaning of 'palace' and 'temple' in both Hebrew and Phoenician), and which was later called the 'Holy Place', and lastly the Debir (roughly, the 'back room') which was later called the 'Holy of the Holies': this was the part reserved to Yahweh, and the Ark of the Covenant stood there.[189]

Biblical Account of the Temple Construction

Before his death, King David had provided materials in great abundance for the building of the temple on the summit of Mount Moriah,[190] where he had purchased a threshing floor from Araunah the Jebusite, on which he offered sacrifice. The Temple was 20 cubits wide: the Ulam was 10 cubits long, the Hekal 40 cubits and the Debir 20 cubits. There is no mention of walls which partitioned it inside, and yet there certainly was one between the Ulam and the Hekal. The Hekal and the Debir are in fact treated as one whole: properly speaking they formed the 'house', the Temple, and together they were 60 cubits long.[191] This is very explicit as it states:

In the beginning of his reign, King Solomon of the United Kingdom of Israel, set about giving effect to the ideas of his father, and prepared additional materials for the building. From subterranean quarries at Jerusalem he obtained huge blocks of stone for the foundations and walls of the temple. These stones were prepared for their places in the building under the eye of Tyrian master-builders. According to this account, Solomon also entered into a compact with Hiram I, king of Tyre, for the supply of whatever else was needed for the work, particularly timber from the forests of Lebanon, which was brought in great rafts by the sea to Joppa, whence it was dragged to Jerusalem.[192]

According to biblical tradition, many thousands of labourers and skilled artisans were employed in the work. Stones prepared in

---

[189] Ibid., 313.

[190] (1 Chronicles 22:14; 29:4; 2 Chronicles 3:1).

[191] Roland de Vaux, *Ancient Israel- Its Life and Institutions*................ 313.

[192] 1 Kings 5.

the quarries underneath the city[193] of huge dimension were gradually placed on the massive walls, and closely fitted together without any mortar between, till the whole structure was completed.[194] In fact, it can be presumed that the Temple of Jerusalem was constructed by certain *vastu* principles,[195] (as the construction of the Temple is based on a Proportion system commanded by Yahweh) which were directed by Yahweh Himself, and was not according to human plan, design or ideas.[196]

Site of the Temple of Jerusalem and its Relevance

Solomon built the house on Mount Moriah,[197] but God had chosen it long before as the mount of sacrifice, when He said to Abraham:

'Take now thy son, thine only son Isaac, whom thou lovest, and get thee into the land of Moriah; and offer him there for a burnt offering.'[198]

Without this offering the types would be incomplete, for Isaac was willing sacrifice, which no animal could be. In the Genesis account we see that God sought Abraham, but here David seeks and finds God in the only appointed way, through sacrifice. The whole place was bought with gold, because the glorious Temple of gold was to be built thereon; but the place of sacrifice was bought with silver, which is always redemption money.[199]

Hence, we notice that the whole temple and its architecture was executed according to the divine intervention and in accordance to certain measures commanded by God and no human intervention

---

[193] 1 Kings 5:17, 18.

[194] Ibid., 314.

[195] Vastu is based on mathematical, geomagnetic, philosophical and metaphysical concepts. These concepts are no abstractions, but living forces which become operative in determining the direction of one's life. The temple of Jerusalem was selected by God Himself, to be His dwelling place.

[196] 1 Kings 6.

[197] The selection of Ornan's threshing floor for building the temple is recorded in 1 Chronicles 21:18-26.

[198] Gen. 22:2.

[199] Arthur E. Smith, *The Temple and Its Teaching* (Chicago: Moody Press, 1956), 27-28.

was made to the Divine plan of the Temple.[200] This Divine proportion system for architecture can be related to the *vastu shastra* in Indian architecture, with special reference to sacred architecture.

Traditional Church Architecture of Kerala

The Church is a place for the gathering of the community for participating in religious services. The disposition of spaces in a Church can be along a longitudinal axis as can be seen in Basilican type of churches or it can also be along a centralized axis.[201] In Kerala, the traditional Church had followed a layout plan with spatial disposition along the longitudinal axis. In plan, it is a long rectangular hall for the congregation, with a Chancel or Sanctum or Altar area, known as the *Madbaha.*[202]

The Churches in Kerala that follows the Eastern tradition have a tripartite plan comprising the *Madbaha, Hykala* and *Kestromo.* While the sanctuary and nave are basic components of the liturgical space in the Syrian tradition, it is in no way a separation between the sacred and the profane, and the clergy and the laity, but a gathering together before the throne of God.[203]

Influence of Persian Church and West Syrian Church Architecture

The Church Architecture of Kerala had developed based on indigenous architectural traditions of the land which in turn had evolved from climatic considerations, social needs and culture of the society. The ideologies of Eastern ecclesiastical traditions also influenced the development of Church Architecture in Kerala,[204]

---

[200] 1 Kings 6.

[201] Anupa Elizba Alex, *Architecture: Space, Issues and Material* (Ahmedabad: CEPT University Press, 2013), 21.

[202] The word 'Madbaha' was derived from the Syrian word 'Dabaha' which means sacrifice. The nave of the church was called the Hykala. It came from Hykalo, the Syrian word meaning 'temple'. Kestromo is the Holy place, just after the madbaha.

[203] Ibid., 22.

[204] Anupa Elizba Alex, Architecture, Space, Issues and Material (Ahmedabad: CEPT University Press, 2013), 23.

because until the sixteenth century the Kerala church had been under the ecclesiastical administration of the East Syrian church.[205]

The built form of churches in Syria or Persia[206] was heavily influenced by the local pagan customs and practices at other Christian centres. By the 4th century C.E, the Christians had two distinct types of ecclesiastical structures - the rectangular basilica for regular liturgy and the centrally oriented churches built as *martyria*[207] and baptistries.[208] Of the characteristic features of the central type of architecture, the dome surprisingly never found its way into Kerala.

The architecture of the Syrian region is dependent on the geological formation of the country and the local materials that were available for construction. In North Syria where limestone was available in abundance, a free stone architecture developed. Since

---

[205] The East Syrian Church or Seleucian church or Chaldean church or Nestorian church or Assyrian church or the Persian church are all one and the same. They say that the Apostle St. Thomas sent Addai to Edessa and that Addai's disciple Mari founded the Church in Seleucia-Ctesiphon. They also say that the Apostle Thomas, before he passed over o India, and also the Apostle Peter visited their Church. The East Syrian Rite which probably had its origin in Edessa developed in the Seleucian church along with the development of that Church. (Placid J. Podippara, *The Thomas Christians...* 37-38).

[206] The tradition of the Malabar church which recounts two events through the first of which this church, founded by the Apostle Thomas, entered into relation with the East Syrian or Chaldean church in the middle of the 4h century, and through the second these relations were further reinforced at the end of the 8th century. Documentary evidence for this tradition is scanty and fragmentary. We have the un-mistakable witness of Cosmos Indicopleustus about Christian communities in Socotora, Ceylon and on the Malabar coast, which lived in relation with the Church of Persia. (A. Mathias Mundadan, *The Arrival of Portuguese in India and The Thomas Christians* (Bangalore: Dharmaram College, 1967), 26). Clear evidence for the hierarchical relation between Malabar and Seleucia, through Persia proper, is furnished by Patriarch Iso'yahb III of Seleucia (628-646) in his letter to Simon of Riwardasir of Persia. (Placid J. Podippara, *The Thomas Christians* (Bombay: St. Paul Publications, 1970), 65).

The Thomas Chistians had relations with the West Syrian Church only in the 17th century, with the arrival of the West Syrian prelate Mar Gregorios in 1665.

[207] M*artyria*- A church or other edifice built at a site, especially a tomb, associated with a Christian martyr or saint.

[208] baptistery- a building next to a church, used for baptism.

the countryside was thickly wooded, a double pitched timber roof covered with tiles was employed as a protection against the heavy winter rains. In South Syria, which was abundant in basalt, the architecture was profoundly affected by the hardness of the stone. The spanning limit of the material was by no means sufficient for a large congregational space and therefore it necessitated the joining together of a number of narrow rooms, the walls being pierced by arches.[209]

Hence, the use of semi-circular arches and vaults were common in the churches in both the East Syrian and West Syrian tradition.[210] The ecclesial relation between the *Malankara* church and the Persian and Syrian churches resulted in the use of arches in church buildings.[211] The lack of windows and thick walls was definitely not a response to the local humid climate, but could have been a direct transplantation of the Semitic building style. Churches of this period lack any ornamentation in the *madbaha,* which could have been due to the prevalent Nestorian or Persian church influence over the churches.[212]

Portuguese Influence

With the arrival of the Portuguese[213] in India, along with colonisation in India, Latinisation of the Church began. The initial ecclesiastical structures built by the Portuguese in Goa were replicas of the Churches in their native land. In already constructed churches, changes were made mainly to the external façade and openings. An important change in spatial organisation was the introduction of

---

[209] Ibid., 25.

[210] Ibid., 25.

[211] Ibid., 19.

[212] Ibid., 11.

[213] The Portuguese Admiral Vasco de Gama landed in Calicut in 1498 and made friends with the Zamorin, the ruler of Calicut. Later evangelisation was carried out everywhere inspite of the resistance by local rulers. The Portuguese thought that the Thomas Christians were under their ecclesiastical jurisdiction. They also wanted to latinize the Thomas Christians and do away with the jurisdiction of the Seleucian Patriarch in Malabar and the other parts of India. (Placid J. Podippara, *The Thomas Christians*......... 119, 122).

secondary altars and the transept for the intermediary choir.[214] The west side tall facades in almost all the churches in *Malankara* was a result of the Latinisation of church architecture. There were no facades for churches before the 15th century. One of the main feature of any European church was its imposing front façade, whereas the indigenous Kerala churches did not have such a feature at all. The 'front wall' was plain, with a tile and wood roof projecting over that it.[215]

The Portuguese who embarked on a policy of Latinisation of the church, also took steps to introduce changes in the plan and ornamentation of the church, along with the idea of God and worship. However, they faced opposition from the local rulers and had to head northwards towards Goa.

Cross Cultural Influences

The first organised religions to reach Kerala were the Jains and the evangelising Buddhist missions of Emperor Ashoka in 300-200 B.C. While Jainism flourished in Kerala till 500 A. D., Buddhism was in vogue till the arrival of Vedic Brahmins in around 800 A.D. So it is quite natural that architectural development of these religions would have also influenced churches of the region.[216]

Unlike Hindu temples, *chaityas*[217] were constructed to host and provide shelter to a large number of devotees, similar to a church. The earliest rock-cut *chaityas* of the Ashokan times, consisted of a rectangular chamber in which worshippers could congregate and a small circular room beyond, with a doomed roof. The form of the inner chamber was governed by the object of worship that was to house - the stupa. With further development of Buddhist rituals, it became necessary to introduce a path for circumambulation which

---

[214] Ibid., 12-13.

[215] Sunil Edward, *A Prelude to the Study of Indigenous, Pre-European, Church Architecture of Kerala* (Trivandrum: Chitkara University, 2014), 172.

[216] Ibid., 21.

[217] A *chaitya* is a Buddhist shrine or prayer hall with a stupa at one end. In modern texts on Indian architecture, the term *chaitya-griha* is often used to denote an assembly or prayer hall that houses a stupa.

led to the construction of a row of pillars dividing the interiors into a central nave and narrow aisles on either side.[218]

By the 8th century A.D., Buddhism and Jainism were replaced by Brahmanical Hinduism as the dominant religion of Kerala. The influence of Hinduism on Syrian Christians is seen not only in the architecture of religious edifices, but also in the rituals and customs. The churches were located on prominent sites, enclosed by compound walls and entered through *padippuramallika.* The compound walls typically followed a pattern similar to temple compound walls with stone lamps embedded in them.[219]

Regional Factors Affecting Architecture

Religious buildings in Kerala have been accorded their importance by positioning them on vantage points as laid down in *sastras.*[220] It has been observed that Jain and Buddhist *chaitayas*, Hindu temples and churches strictly adhere to this tradition of strategic placement. In hilly areas, the churches are generally built on the highest location so as to occupy a commanding position. (eg. Kottayam Valiyapalli and Kadamattompalli). This has got a Biblical basis; the temple of Jerusalem built by Solomon, was built on Mount Moriah at the command of Yahweh. There is also a Theological connotation for this. An ascent to a height means a spiritual elevation; e.g. Moses' ascending Mount Sinai. Steps (*padikettu*) made either of stone or laterite is provided on all or some sides of the church and they add to the grandeur and beauty of the church building. In lowlands, churches are generally located on the river banks or near shores since waterways were the main mode of transport in the olden days.[221]

---

[218] Ibid., 21.

[219] Ibid., 23.

[220] *sastras-* is a Sanskrit word that means "precept, rules, manual, compendium, book or treatise" in a generalsense. The word is generally used as a suffix in the Indian literature context, for technical or specialized knowledge in a defined area of practice

[221] Ibid., 18-19.

Vastu Vidya in Ancient Church Architecture of Kerala

When studying the features of the architecture and *vastu vidya* of ancient churches in Kerala, there are three important patterns of construction:

1. South Indian Style
2. Persian Style
3. Western Style

The South-Indian style is the matter of scope for this study and the details of which are furnished below. By South-Indian style we mean the *Vastu* style that is prevalent in Kerala. The early churches built in Kerala very much resembled the outward pattern of Hindu temples. There are altars which are square shaped, the *stupa* shaped *mandapa* and *dwaja stamba*[222] etc., in ancient churches. The *gopura*[223] or tall spire above the sanctuary of churches, might be an imitation of the *shikara*[224] above the *girbha grha* of temples. There are rock crosses mounted on rock base in old churches which resembled the *balikallu* in Hindu temples. The belfry and *mukhappu*[225] above the *madbaha*

---

[222] *Dhwaja Stambha*, or Flag Pole, is an important feature of most South Indian Temples. *Dhwaja Stambha* is installed in front of the temple.

[223] Gopuram is a monumental tower, usually ornate, at the entrance of any temple, especially in Southern India. This forms a prominent feature of Koils, Hindu temples of the Dravidian style. They are topped by the kalasam, a bulbous stone finial.

[224] Shikhara, (Sanskrit: "mountain peak") also spelled shikara, also called shikar, in North Indian temple architecture, the superstructure, tower, or spire above the sanctuary and also above the pillared mandapas (porches or halls); it is the most dominant and characteristic feature of the Hindu temple in the north India. (https://www.britannica.com/technology/shikhara)

[225] Mukhappu-is the front portion of the gabled roof of old buildings in Kerala.

of church is very much similar to the *vimana*[226] construction above the *sreekovil* (Sanctuary) of Hindu temple.[227]

The ancient Christian churches had similarities with Hindu temples for the following reasons:

1. There was no basic plan for the church in Kerala in the early centuries.[228]
2. The craftsmen and skilled workers who built churches were those who built temples and they were Hindus. It is obvious that the idea of sacred place known to them is that of Hindu temples. Thus, it is quite evident that churches were built according to certain *vastu* principles, that which was applicable for temple construction too.[229] The Anthimalankavu church at Kunnamkulam, Kalloopara church and the Chengannur Old Syrian church are best examples of Kerala *vastu vidya* traditional construction.[230]

Generally, all the old and important temples in Kerala have been built on prominent sites and most of the temples are situated on the outskirts of the village, concealed behind compound walls with a pond nearby. The best example is the one at Padmanabhapuram Temple at Thiruvananthapuarm. The churches of the Middles Ages (6th – 16th C. E) are fine examples of churches resembling Hindu temples in the layout of the complex as well as in their overall appearance. Kalloopara St. Mary's church and Anthimalankavu church at Kunnamkulam are examples. The churches were also located on prominent sites, though within the heart of the village or

---

[226] Vimāna is a mythological flying palace or chariot described in Hindu texts and Sanskrit epics. The Pushpaka Vimana of the demon king Ravana (which was taken from Lord Kubera, and returned to him by Rama) is the most quoted example of a vimana. Vimanas are also mentioned in Jain texts.

[227] Mohanakshan Nair A., *Vasthuvidya Christhava-Muslim Devalayangal* (Kottayam: D C Press (P) Ltd., 2009), 32-33.

[228] Ibid., 32.

[229] Ibid., 33.

[230] Ibid., 33.

town, enclosed by compound walls and entered through *padippura malika* (entrance gateway).[231]

The three-tier gabled indigenous architecture of Kerala churches, which lacked facades until the coming of the Portuguese, immensely gains in richness symmetry, and beauty because of the open-air rock crosses, some of them more than 30 feet in height including the intricately carved pedestals, and monolithic shafts. No other community in Kerala has such a huge monumental stone structure. The indoor counterparts of these crosses have the earliest carvings in Kerala of the national flower lotus and the national bird peacock. Perhaps even the national animal tiger is first depicted in Kerala art in church sculpture. There was no rock carving in South India prior to the period of these indoor crosses. The motifs, message, and images on these crosses and their pedestals display a remarkable degree of Indianness.[232]

The base with a socket, the monolithic square and slightly tapering shaft with cylindrical terminals, the horizontal piece forming the arms with a double (hole) socket in the middle, and the capital with a cylindrical bottom end are the four members of the open air cross. They are so well chiselled and proportionate that when put together the socket and cylinder arrangement enables the cross to stand by itself. However for the bigger crosses, pedestals in the form of sacrificial alters of *Ballikallus* are found, often carrying exquisite reliefs of the flora and fauna of the land in addition to scenes from daily life and biblical scenes.[233]

Indigenous Church Architecture of Kerala

Orientation

The Orientation of the traditional Kerala Church is always in the East–West axis with the *Madbaha* on the East, and the main entry to the Church on the West. This was so, irrespective of the orientation of the site, the road or river access.

---

[231] Anupa Elizba Alex, *Architecture: Space, Issues and Material* (Ahmedabad: CEPT University Press, 2013), 23.

[232] Ibid.

[233] Ibid.

Characteristics of Indigenous Church Architecture of Kerala[234]

1. Focus towards the altar.
2. Once the main door is crossed the focus is always toward the Altar.
3. Constricted *Madbaha.*
   The *Madbaha* part of the indigenous Church is always shorter in width than that of the *Hykala.*
4. Higher roof for the *Madbaha.*
   The roof of the *Madbaha* was always higher than that of the *Hykala.*
5. Windows/Doors.
   Madbaha did not have windows. There were three doors to the *Hykala.* The main door is accessed from the west. The two side doors are one each on the north and south side. The number of windows were minimal or nil.
6. Additional roof above the *Madbaha*
   The *Madbaha* had double roof. The lower one is a highly decorated vaulted roof above the altar. This vaulted roof is covered by a raised hipped or pitched roof, which is seen from outside.
   Arch opening between the *Madbaha* and *Hykala Madbaha* and *Hykala* are separated by an arched opening.

Summary

This chapter highlighted the major aspects of *vastu vidya* in Indian culture and the architectural traditions of the churches of Kerala. The study includes the principles of *vastu* for sacred space, the *vastu* of temples, and spatial organisation of the temple of Jerusalem. The influence of East Syrian and West Syrian church architecture on the church architecture of Kerala is also discussed.

---

[234] S. Panjikaran, R. Vedamuthu, *An Evaluation of Spatial Organization of the Church Architecture of Keraladuring the Sixteenth to Seventeenth Centuries,* The Institution of Engineers (India), 2013 (30 October 2013), http://paperity.org/p/36563323/an-evaluation-of-spatial-organization-of-the-church-architecture-of-kerala-during-the Sixteenth to Seventeenth centuries (24 Feb. 2017).

Vastu shastra or the science of architectural procedures that is prevalent in South India especially in Kerala presents an age old heritage of our land and culture. Even though, the *vastu shastra* has its roots in the *puranas and vedas* and the native Hindu temples were built with these principles, it has greatly influenced the architecture of Christian churches too.

Churches that existed in the sixteenth century in Kerala were subjected to renovation by the Portuguese and missionaries. The new space requirements that arose due to the change in liturgy, was incorporated into the indigenous church plan without making any drastic changes in that plan. The new churches that were built during this period were of two types. Churches that resembled the indigenous plan and the churches that varied from the indigenous churches in terms of spatial layout. Churches in both these types incorporated the indigenous characters as well as the architectural characters imported from the west. The missionaries tried to transfer their ideas into the built form with the help of the local artisans and craftsmen, who were well versed in the indigenous techniques and construction practices. The result was the architectural expression of ideas imported from the West reflected on a foreground developed based on the architectural traditions of the East. It can be concluded that the influx of Western ideologies has tried to enhance the Church Architecture of Kerala in the sixteenth century. Nevertheless, enrichments made in terms of spatial organization and architectural character did not overthrow its indigenous character, developed based on Eastern and Western ecclesiastical traditions.

Chapter 3

The Architecture of Selected Ancient Syrian Churches in Kerala

An introspection into the architecture of ancient churches in Kerala reveals a bunch of theological facts, which can be established, based on the scripture. All the ancient churches in Kerala has got many elements in common and the structures bears close resemblance with each other and the native Hindu temples, even though the influence of the Portuguese brought about new patterns and facades for the indigenous churches of Kerala. The vivid theological elements open new spiritual insights and spiritual experiences which leads us to an atmosphere conducive to worship. This chapter is a humble attempt to go into the depth of signs, symbols and theological facts, to some extent, prevalent in church architecture of selected ancient Syrian churches of Kerala namely Thiruvithamcode St. Mary's church, Kallooppara St. Mary's church and Kaduthuruthy St. Mary's church.

Selected Ancient Syrian Churches

The selected ancient Syrian churches are in a geographical area across the erstwhile state of Travancore,[235] and many of the local

[235] The Kingdom of Travancore was an Indian kingdom from 1729 until 1949. It was ruled by the Travancore Royal Family from Padmanabhapuram, and later

characteristics are prevalent in the structures of this specific locality. Three churches namely Thiruvithamcode St. Mary's church, Kallooppara St. Mary's church and Kaduthuruthy St. Mary's church. These three churches were selected on the basis of their locations. The first church is situated in the southern part of Kerala (now in Kanyakumari district of Tamil Nadu; this region was part of erstwhile Tranvancore before the formation of Kerala state). The second church, Kallooppara St. Mary's church is situated in the central Travancore and the third one Kaduthuruthy St. Mary's church is at a north central part of Kerala. This selection based on location was intended for understanding the construction practices of churches and the theological elements involved in the architecture prevalent in different parts of Kerala in the ancient times, especially in the Pre-Portuguese period.

St. Mary's Orthodox Church, Thiruvithamcode

Historical Background

This ancient and one of the oldest existing church in Christendom is believed to be established by St. Thomas, one of the twelve Apostles' of Jesus Christ in 63 CE. The present church structure, which is mainly made out of rock, dates back to around 558 CE. The church is locally known as *arapally* meaning king's church, was a privilege given to the church in the first century by the king of the erstwhile *Chera* province.[236] The church is also called *Thomayar Kovil* which

---

Thiruvananthapuram. At its zenith, the kingdom covered most of modern-day central and southern Kerala with the Thachudaya Kaimal's enclave of Irinjalakuda in the neighbouring Kingdom of Cochin, as well as the district of Kanyakumari, now in the Indian state of Tamil Nadu.

[236] The Cheras were an ancient Dravidian royal dynasty of Tamil origin. The first to establish an historical ruling dynasty in the area, they ruled wide-ranging areas of Tamil Nadu and Kerala in south-eastern and south-western India respectively, areas that had been settled since at least 5000 BC, when Neolithic carvings had been left in Edakkal Caves. Chera territory included regions such as Venad, Kuttanad, Kudanad, Pazhinad, and others, encompassing the area between Kanyakumari in the south to Kasargod in the north (now in the far north of Kerala). Also included in this list are Palghat, Coimbatore, Salem and Kollimalai, although they quite probably did not rule all of these areas at all times as ancient borders could be quite fluid at times. Their core territory was in Kerala, while the later rise of the Pallavas

means the temple of St. Thomas, situated in Kanyakumari district of Tamil Nadu state near to Thiruvananthapuram- Nagercoil highway. Even though small in size, the ancient church brings out many architectural, theological and cultural elements that were prevalent in the early centuries in this locality.[237]

In not only Thiruvithamcode church but in all the other churches built by St. Thomas in India, there wasn't a structure as we see today. The ancient structure might be only a basic structure for the celebration of the Eucharist. It should have been an altar made of rock as Patriarch Jacob and Prophet Elijah, in the Old Testament times, did for an offering[238] to God. The ancient churches of the early centuries in Kerala where small structures made of the locally available material, to shelter from rain, sunlight, etc. In due course of time the floor, permanent roof, strong walls, etc., evolved for churches. We can presume that the present altar of the church has the stones which St. Thomas used for making an altar. Apart from the altar stones, the other materials used might be bamboo, palm leaves, thatched coconut leaves, grass, etc.[239]

Basically Christian churches were built exclusively for the purpose of celebrating the Holy Eucharist in the early centuries. Sacraments like baptism was conducted in churches only after many centuries. In such a background churches where built in the same manner as that of the *Girbhagrha* of Hindu temples which was small in size. This is what is reflecting inThiruvithamcode church.[240] To this small sanctuary was a small hall or *mandapa* for the worshippers to stand, which was nothing but four columns with a roof surmounting them. As granite was locally available in plenty and the available

---

pushed them out of Tamil Nadu. However, they did establish a capital at Vanchi, which was known by the Romans as Muzris after an active sea-borne trade sprang up between the two powers.

[237] Kurian Thomas K., *Thomayar Kovil- Thiruvithamcode Arachapally* (Kottayam: The Malankara Orthodox Church Publications, 2013), 63.

[238] Genesis 28:10; I Kings 18:20

[239] Kurian Thomas K., *Thomayar Kovil- Thiruvithamcode Arachapally*.........75.

[240] Ibid., 75.

workmanship, all these structures including the roof was made out of granite. This basic plan in still existing and is not altered.[241]

Architecture of Thiruvithamcode Church

Exterior Features

1. Roof: The roof of the church was flat shaped. Large granite pieces 10 feet long and 1 feetwide where laid on the top of the granite wall. There is a clear evidence for this; the granite side walls have got grooves in it, which is intended for the long granite slabs to fit in. But this roof was demolished a century ago as it was in a dilapidated condition.[242] The present gabled roof was put up after this.

2. *Poomukham*: Or the entrance is situated at the west side of the church is a recently built one, with wooden louvered porch in typical Travancore style, and according to *vastu shastra*, similar to but less ornate than the type seen in the nearby Padmanabhapuram palace. The *poomukham* which is 12 feet long is comparatively longer than *poomukhams* in other churches. The six stone pillars support a wooden beam, which transfers the load of the wooden roof.

Signs and Symbols in Poomukham: In the case of Thiruvithamcode church *poomukham* plays a mediatory role between outside world and inner sanctuary. It reinforces the transitional nature of spiritual life. In the early western churches, the atrium preceding the church proper, was associated with the basin for ablution or fountain. The catechumens and those under penance remained here. The *poomukham* provides a space to pause and prepare oneself for worship before entering the church. It allows a glimpse of the divine interior with its candles, lamps and chanting.[243]

3. Front Elevation-Façade: The façade at the west side is comparatively lower than other huge ones in other churches and this is only a century old; built at the time of renovation, during

---

[241] Ibid., 76.

[242] Kurian Thomas K., *Thomayar Kovil-Thiruvithamcode Arachapally*.........67.

[243] Anupa Elizba Alex, *Architecture: Space, Issues and Material* (Ahmedabad: CEPT University Press, 2013), 13.

the 1930's.[244] Another interesting fact about this church according to Fabian Corrage as mentioned by Kurian Thomas is that the Thiruvithamcode church is built in the same plan as that of the Temple of Jerusalem built by Solomon; the front elevation and even the dimensions of both is proportionate in many aspects. No other church in the world owes such a criteria for comparison.[245]

4. Ornate Columns: In the *hykala* portion of the church is four columns or pillars made out of granite, simple in ornamentation with built-in lamps. These columns resembles the ones at Hindu temples but is without ornamentation. These aids in strengthening the structure at the four corners of the *mandapa.*

Signs and Symbols in Ornate Columns: In the nave portion we observe four square shaped stone columns with stone lamps, just as we see in Hindu temples, is according to *vastu*[246] principles.[247] This again gives the notion of the four eternal life giving gospels of the New Testament. Ornamentation is less and similar to that found in early temples.

5. Steps: In Thiruvithamcode church we observe a flight of three steps leading to the hykala from the northern and southern side. In *Vastu Vidya, sopanam*[248] "*kaivarikallu*" means a small stairway from the main door to the ground with a width of 1.5 or 2 feet. All the steps are equally spaced and are usually even numbered. Usually, according to *Vastu Vidya, sopanam* is built at the doorstep of the

---

[244] Ibid., 68.

[245] Ibid., 68.

[246] Similarly, the lengths, the breadths the heights of various elements of the temple too are related to each other by certain ratios. These lend esthetic appeal and stability to the temple structure. For instance, it is said, by restricting the height of the tower, Shikhara, to twice its width at the base, the weight of the tower is contained within itself. Further, as the size of the pada (bay, distance between two pillars) increases, the cross section of pillars also increases in size and width of beam has to be exactly same as that of the pillar.

(Sreenivasarao S, *Temple Architecture Devalaya Vastu,* http://creative.sulekha.com/temple-architecture-devalaya-vastu-part-five-5-of-7_336238_blog (21 Mar. 2017).

[247] Ibid., 79.

[248] The word *Sopanam* refers to the sacred steps of main shrine of a temple.

main shrine- '*srikovil*' in Indian temples. It is evident that the idea of *sopanam* has crept into the construction of churches with regard to steps ascending to the Holy of the Holies, as the local artisans introduced these common elements in Hindu temples as well as Christian churches.[249]

Interior Features

1. *Madbaha*: The church is very small in size with dimensions 20.7m × 5.7m. The *Madbaha* measures 3.50m × 3.88m and houses the altar at a distance of about 0.60m detached from the eastern wall. It has two small windows (*kilivathil*), one each on the north and south wall of the sanctuary. A crude arch, which seems to have been built recently, defines the entry to the *madbaha*. A false ceiling of wood panelling is provided over the altar at the sanctuary.

Signs and Symbols Concerning the *Madbaha:* The east-west axis is of great importance in the churches of Syrian tradition. Irrespective of the orientation of the entry to the church, the *madbaha* is always situated in the east end in accordance with the Eastern Church tradition. The whole congregation along with the celebrants face the east during community worship. Facing east has several biblical reasons, of which the church awaiting the second coming of the Lord from the east is most important.[250] "For as the lightning comes from the east and shines as far as west, so will be the coming of the Son of Man.[251]

The interior of the *madbaha* and the nave is dark even during daytime. Alva William Steffler states that biblically darkness has a range of meanings. In Genesis it is the symbol of primeval chaos (1:2). Physical darkness is also a metaphor for spiritual darkness[252]

---

[249] Rev. Dr. Abraham Mulamootil, *The Tent of the Pilgrim of Exile* (Thiruvalla: Peacepeopleplanet.org, 2016), 76.

[250] Ibid., 9.

[251] St. Matthew 24:27.

[252] 2 Sam. 22:29; Isa. 9:2.

demonstrated by nature at the Crucifixion.[253] Interestingly, the mysterious side of God is referred to as darkness.[254]

In the domestic vernacular architecture of Kerala, indirect diffused light was preferred to the harsh blinding sunlight entering the interiors. Notions of light as a statement of the divine presence, has undergone a series of transformation under varying influences. The Hindu traditions do not consider light as directly representative of divine energy. The religious architecture is guided by two attitudes towards the sacred; one stresses on the mystery aspect-the veiling. Here, the Divine is hidden from the profane. This attitude is prevalent in the Eastern Orthodox churches. On the contrary, in the West, the glory and splendour of the Divine is more stressed upon. In the early Syrian churches the *mabbaha* was a dark cellar evoking images of a *girbhagriha.* The use of lamps, incense and bells in rituals transformed the dark interiors in a very mystic environment, giving a notion of heaven which cannot be demystified by mortals.[255]

According to the Mystical Theology of St. Dionysius the Areopagite:[256]

> Supernal Triad, Deity above all essence, knowledge and goodness; Guide of Christians to Divine Wisdom; direct our path to the ultimate summit of Thy mystical Lore, most incomprehensible, most luminous and most exalted, where the pure, absolute and immutable mysteries of theology are veiled in the dazzling obscurity of the secret Silence, outshining all

---

[253] St. Mark 15:33; St. Luke 23:44

[254] Alva William Steffler, *Symbols of the Christian Faith* (Grand Rapids, Michigan: William B. Eerdmans Publishing Company, 2002), 107; Exo. 19:16; 2 Sam.22:10-12; 1 Kings 8:12: 2 Chron. 6:1; Ps. 18:11; 97:2; Heb. 12:18

[255] Anupa Elizba Alex, *Architecture: Space, Issues and Material*........ 19.

[256] Dionysius the Areopagite was a judge of the Areopagus who, as related in the Acts of the Apostles, was converted to Christianity by the preaching of the Apostle Paul during the Areopagus sermon. Dionysius, or Pseudo-Dionysius, as he has come to be known in the contemporary world, was a Christian Neo-Platonist who wrote in the late fifth or early sixth century CE and who transposed in a thoroughly original way the whole of Pagan Neo-Platonism from Plotinus to Proclus, but especially that of Proclus and the Platonic Academy in Athens, into a distinctively new Christian context.

> brilliance with the intensity of their Darkness, and surcharging our blinded intellects with the utterly impalpable and invisible fairness of glories surpassing all beauty.[257]

Unknowing, or *agnosia,*[258] is not ignorance or nescience[259] as ordinarily understood, but rather the realization that no finite knowledge can fully know the Infinite One, and that therefore it is only truly to be approached by *agnosia,* or by that which is beyond and above knowledge. There are two main kinds of darkness: the sub darkness and the super-darkness, between which lies, as it were, an octave of light. But the nether-darkness and the Divine Darkness are not the same darkness, for the former is absence of light, while the latter is excess of light. The one symbolizes mere ignorance, and the other a transcendent unknowing - a super knowledge not obtained by means of the discursive reason.[260]

The Cappadocian Father St. Gregory of Nyssa in his work 'The Life of Moses" says:

> Since Moses was alone, by having been stripped as it were of the people's fear, he boldly approached the very darkness itself and entered the invisible things where he was no longer seen by those watching. After he entered the inner sanctuary of the divine mystical doctrine, there, while not being seen, he was in company with the Invisible. He teaches, I think, by the things he did that the one who is going to associate intimately with God must go beyond all that is visible and—lifting up his own mind, as to a mountaintop, to the invisible and incomprehensible—believe that the divine is there where the understanding does not reach.[261]

---

[257] Joseph H. Peterson ed., *The Mystical Theology of Dionysius the Areopagite* (England: The Grade city Press Ltd., 2004), http://www.esotericarchives.com/oracle/dionys1.htm (20 Feb. 2017).

[258] Agnosia-inability to interpret sensations and hence to recognize things, typically as a result of brain damage.

[259] Nescience-The doctrine that nothing is actually knowable.

[260] Ibid.

[261] Abraham J. Malherbe, Everett Ferguson, tr., *The Life of Moses* (New York: Paulist Press, 1978), 26.

Gregory's concept of mystical knowing is best expressed in his image of the divine darkness: a symbol that is perhaps one of his greatest gifts to the realm of Christian thought. One must begin a discussion of the divine darkness with an acknowledgement that, in Gregory's writing, it is not the only way of knowing. Indeed, it is not even the first. In the story of Moses, Gregory makes plain the fact that much indeed preceded the patriarch's ascent of Sinai. So, too, must much precede the Christian's entrance into the darkness of Divine Knowledge.[262]

2. Thronos: Or the altar is placed at a distance of 0.60m from the east wall of the church. But earlier, a century ago, it was placed on the east side wall.[263]

3. Arch: Or the vault-presently there is a crude arch at the entrance to the *madbaha* which was made a century ago. Earlier there was no arch at the entrance to the *madbaha* as the roof was at a low level and flat shaped rather than gabled.

4. *Kestromo*: It is 4.70m × 2.05m in size and accommodates the baptismal font on the southern side and the prayer table at the centre. It is raised 0.26m above the *hykala* and is separated from it by railings. At the *kestromo*, just below the *madbaha* there is a cross carved on the stone wall as a relief. This is something noteworthy because in no other portion of the church we see the bas-relief of the cross in the rock structure.

5. *Hykala*: It occurs in two segments as its width reduced at a distance of 4.86m from the *madbaha*. The eastern side of the *hykala* measures 4.7m in width, whereas the western side is only 3.58m wide. Three doors open in to the *hykala*, with the main door on the western wall. The small doors have stone thresholds and are accessed by *sopanam*[264] type steps emulating the temple style. The wooden windows are of a later addition.

---

[262] Ibid., 26.

[263] Kurian Thomas K., *Thomayar Kovil-Thiruvithamcode Arachapally......* 76.

[264] Sopanam- steps leading to the Sanctuary in Hindu temples.

Signs and Symbols in *Hykala:* The hykala is likened to a ship or Noah's ark which saved God's chosen people. It also symbolizes the area where the sons of Israel congregated when Moses went up Mount Sinai.[265]

6. Doors: Small sized doors is a specialty of this church. Small doors on the sides makes one's entry into the church bowing. This is a way of adoration to God before entering the house of God, an Eastern way of adoration respectful gesture.

Signs and Symbols Concerning Doors: In the case of the provision of door, it was few in number in ancient churches of Kerala. The steps of the *madbaha (sanctuary)* and the west side door were considered as entrances. But single doors were present at the south, north and west sides of the church building. Each of these doors have got a symbolism: the West door represents Mercy, South represents Repentance and the Northern door represents Hope. All these have got Christian and biblical importance. The door at the East is the door of Glory and which is never opened. This is the reason why there isn't a door, as such, at the eastern side of the church.[266] The door also represents hope,[267] opportunity,[268] and the entrance into the Kingdom of God.[269] The door also represent transition to a new state of being, such as the after life. In architectural symbology, the three doors of a cathedral stand for faith, hope and charity.[270]

7. Small Windows: We find two very small windows with a pointed Gothic arch at top, and the windows measures 20cm in height and 15cm wide which are placed at the centre of the northern and southern walls of the sanctuary. Scientifically his aids in cross-ventilation; but this has theological connotations too.

---

[265] Ibid., 59.

[266] Ibid., 49.

[267] Hos. 2:15.

[268] 1 Cor. 16:9; Rev. 3:8.

[269] Matt. 25:10; Luke 13:25; Rev. 3:8; 4:1.

[270] Alva William Steffler, *Symbols of the Christian Faith* (Grand Rapids, Michigan: Wm. B. Eerdmans Publishing Co., 2002), 62.

Signs and Symbols Concerning Windows: Small Windows at the Sanctuary-theologically this has a connotation. The early church Fathers like Origen compared the church building metaphorically to Noah's ark, which was built by God's command and which saved Noah and his family with all birds and animals two by two, male and female. Noah's ark is a symbolism for salvation.[271] The two small windows can be presumed to be the small window of the ark which was insisted by God;

'You shall make a window for the ark, and you shall finish it to a cubit from above; and set the door of the ark in its side; you shall make it with lower, second, and third decks.'[272] No detail of the Genesis flood account is insignificant for patristic interpreters like Augustine. For example, in Genesis 6 we are told that, in addition to the door on the side, Noah was instructed to make an "opening" for daylight, presumably near the top of the ark. Then, he was ordered to "finish the ark a cubit about it"[273] Another important fact is that Noah's faith also saved the animals;[274] the whole creation will be saved through the children of God.[275]

It is quite interesting to note Jean Danielou's quote from a Homily of Clement of Rome, according to which:

The body of the Church as a whole is like a great ship carrying men of many different origins through a violent storm. There follows a long allegory, in which God is the owner of the ship and Christ the captain, the bishop is like the look-out man, the presbyters are the crew, the deacons the leading oarsmen, the catechists the stewards.[276]

8. Ornamentations: In Thiruvithamcode church we find minimal ornamentation, but on very close observation we find traces of such

---

[271] The Orthodox Study Bible- Commentary on Genesis 6, p. 12.

[272] Genesis 6:16.

[273] Stephen Beale, *Ten Ways Noah's Ark Prefigured the Church*- Catholic Exchange (Mar. 24' 2014) http://catholicexchange.com/ten-ways-noahs-ark-prefigured-church (24 Feb. 2017).

[274] Gen. 7:2-15.

[275] Rom. 8:18-22.

[276] Jean Danielou, *Primitive Christian Symbols* (London: Spottiswoode Ballantyne and Co. Ltd, 1961), 58.

works on the granite walls. These are not at all clear; which might be because of the age of the structure, with age many an image have lost their clarity.

9. Bas-relief: The main western door has a plate with bas-reliefs[277] above it in stone depicting either side of a chalice and bread used for Holy Eucharist. This points out the fact that there was the practice of celebrating the Holy Eucharist and that was the customary.

Signs and Symbols in Bas-relief: The *madbaha* is devoid of any images or ornamentation and can be attributed to the early Nestorian belief[278] which was prevalent. The main western door has a stone plate with bas-reliefs above it in stone depicting two angels, chalice and bread used for Eucharist. On the wall adjacent to the *madbaha*, there exists a cross as relief on rock wall, which is the only cross on the whole structure. On the exterior walls, at lintel level we observe gargoyles[279] in the shape of serpents, which definitely is a result of local architectural influences.

10. Baptismal Font: Inside the church we find a small baptismal font made of granite which has a diameter of just 22cm mounted on a granite pedestal. This gives us a presumption that this small font was used for baptizing infants. Inside the *kestromo* we can observe a large granite font which is of recent origin. Another granite font is found outside the church on the north side below the door at that side. The striking feature of this font is the presence of a relief of a cross on it and this itself gives us all proof that it is a font used for baptism.

11. Granite Cross: To the west side of the church, below the plot where the church is situated is a huge granite cross twelve feet in height. The present cross is a new one, installed a couple of years ago;

---

[277] Bas-Relief is a sculptural technique where the sculpted elements remain attached to a solid background of the same material. The term relief is from the Latin verb *relevo*, to raise. To create a sculpture in relief is to give the impression that the sculpted material has been raised above the background plane.

[278] The Nestorian Church belief is that the use of images breaks the second commandment of God.

[279] gargoyle- a grotesque carved human or animal face or figure projecting from the gutter of a building, typically acting as a spout to carry water clear of a wall.

but it its position there existed an old shrine with a cross, the age of which is unknown.

St. Mary's Orthodox Church, Kallooppara

Historical Background

Kallooppara was part of 'Thekkumkore' kingdom. The land Kallooppara was given as a gift by the King of Edapally. The serene village upon the banks of river Manimala was known as 'Perumpranad' meaning the land of huge rock. People from Kuravilangad, Vaikom and Kadampanad, which were the then Christian prominent places, migrated to Kallooppara centuries back. They had to reach the Niranam church for worship and for other sacraments. It was very tedious for them to reach Niranam church, sailing through rivers Manimala and Pamba. Realizing their plight the king granted permission to erect a church on the bank of the river. The generosity of the king eventually brought about a sense of unity among the Christians of Kallooppara. The place given by the king had been known as *Thamarassery illam* lying west to the Kallooppara Devi temple.[280]

St. Mary's Orthodox Syrian Church, situated at the heart of a small village called Kallooppara (on the banks of the river Manimalayar), Pathanamthitta District, is a prized possession of Malankara Orthodox Church. The church has a legacy of around seven centuries, keeping its tradition and culture intact without compromising on its religious values. The church is an elegant representation of the beautiful shingled[281] roof tops in the early Kerala style. The present church was built in 1339 AD.[282] The church is a perfect example of the ancient temple architecture and is a mystery the way it has overcome all the challenges of time. The sanctorium that is abstract in all aspects is a mystifying beauty of the ancient architecture, which has a keen and splendid blend of beauty and

---

[280] Fr. C. K. Kurien, ed., *Kallooppara Valiya Palli- Sahashrabda Smaranika* .... 37.

[281] Shingle- a thin piece of wood, slate, metal, asbestos, or the like, usually oblong, laid in overlapping rows to cover the roofs and walls of buildings.

[282] Joseph V. Thomas, *Charithram Urangunna Kallooppara Palliyum Thilangunna Asthikalum* (Kottayam: Graphic Zone, 2000), 76.

science in it. This is one of the rare churches built in the traditional '*Thachusastra*'[283] style, deeply rooted in the ancient Kerala culture.

Architecture of Kallooppara St. Mary's Orthodox Church

Exterior Features

1. Roof: Among the few churches in Kerala that has very close resemblance to Hindu temple, Kallooppara church is one of them. The external feature of the roof, the gabled roof[284] is the same which is provided in Hindu temples. The purlins and rafters laid according to a particular angle of the gable corresponds to certain fixed *vastu and thachu sastra* principles, which is usually followed in local Hindu temples.

Signs and Symbols Concerning Roof: The roof of the sanctuary is at a higher level than the roof of the other portion of the church building. The raised roof and the *madbaha* signifies that it is the heaven existing above, and its glory. The different colours used to decorate the ornate boards represents the grandeur and spiritual illumination of the place.[285]

2. Poomukham: The church conforms to the ancient temple architecture prevalent in Kerala. Apart from the newly erected *poomukhams* at the south and west sides there are only two

---

[283] Kerala architecture is a kind of architectural style that is mostly found in Indian state of Kerala and all the architectural wonders of Kerala stands out to be ultimate testimonials for the ancient vishwakarma sthapathis of Kerala. Kerala's style of architecture is unique in India, in its striking contrast to Dravidian architecture which is normally practiced in other parts of South India. The architecture of Kerala has been influenced by Dravidian and Indian Vedic architectural science (Vastu Shastra) over two millennium. The Tantrasamuchaya, Thachu-Shastra, Manushyalaya-Chandrika and Silparatna are important architectural sciences, which have had a strong impact in Kerala Architecture style. The Manushyalaya-Chandrika, a work devoted to domestic architecture is one such science which has its strong roots in Kerala.

[284] A gable is the generally triangular portion of a wall between the edges of intersecting roof pitches. The shape of the gable and how it is detailed depends on the structural system used, which reflects climate, material availability, and aesthetic concerns.

[285] Op cit., 19.

poomukhams for the church. The ones at the south and west sides were constructed during the renovation period.[286] The present plan of the church proper consists of the *madbaha, qestromo, hykala and five poomukams,*[287] two each at the southern and northern sides and one at the western side below the façade. The *poomukham* on the northern side is the oldest and the main entry to the church. Stone columns support an ornately carved pitched wooden roof. Bas-reliefs of angels, animals, human figures are carved on column posts and plinth.[288] Details are furnished in architecture of Thiruvithamcode church.

3. Ornate Columns: The eighty feet long verandahs that run on either side of the church has got numerous ornate columns that exhibit designed capitals and bases. The various *poomukhams,* entablature architraves, the wooden carvings inside the church, etc., reveal the greatness and magnificence of the Keralite '*thachu sastra*' and '*vastu vidya*'. There is also a '*Pally meda*'[289] at the northern side of the church in the first floor, near to the *poomukham.* The roof of the verandahs are made of ornately designed cloisters[290] above which comes the rafters atop which the roof tiles are laid. The cloister points out the fact that it involves *vasthu satra* for its installation.[291]

4. Front Elevation-Façade: On the west side stands as an edifice of grandeur and aesthetic beauty. According to the history of the church, the façade was the result of the Portuguese Church influence.[292] There is the victorious cross at the summit of the façade spire and below which are the images of St. Mary, St. Peter, St. Paul, angels blowing trumpets, fish, lamb, etc.

---

[286] 1997-2008.

[287] Poomukham- It is the prime portico soon after steps to the building. Traditionally it has a slope tiled roof with pillars supporting roof. Sides are open.

[288] Fr. C. K. Kurien, ed., *Kallooppara Valiya Palli- Sahashrabda Smaranika*.. 37.

[289] Pallymeda- buildindg or a room adjacent to the church building for Bishops and Priests to rest.

[290] Cloister-a covered walk in a convent, monastery, college, or cathedral, typically with a colonnade open to a quadrangle on one side.

[291] Fr. C. K. Kurien, ed., *Kallooppara Valiya Palli- Sahashrabda Smaranika*..... 37.

[292] Ibid., 25.

Signs and Symbols Concerning Façade: The facades built at the west side is at a soaring height with the sign of victory, the cross, at the topmost end. This represents the ascent of a believer to a high position to experience the glory of God, once you enter the church building. The main entrance to the church building is provided at the west side at the centre. This has a theological connotation; the moment we turn towards the Lord, the veil is removed and hence the entry into the House of the Lord should facilitate the vision of the sanctuary, without any hindrance, where the incarnational mysteries are celebrated.[293]

5. Bas-relief: On the beautifully adorned façade on the west side of the church, we observe bas-relief of various images like eagle, St. Mary, St. Peter, angels blowing trumpets, Fish and lamb, each of which has a symbolism.

Signs and Symbols in Bas-relief

Eagle: On the top portion. Just below the main cross of the façade is the image of an eagle.The eagle is a repeated motif in the visions found in Ezekial and revelation[294] Saint Jerome assigned the symbol of the eagle to John the Gospel writer "because his Gospel opens with 'in the beginning was the Word' thus carrying the reader into the Heavenlies". The eagle is also a symbol of a soaring, rejuvenated spirit (Ps.103:5) and the soul strengthened by God's grace (Is.40:31). It also represents divine inspiration, which is why lecterns where the Word of God is read are designed in the shape of an eagle with outstretched wings. When an eagle grows old and its eyes are failing, it flies towards the sun so that the blinding film is burned away from its eyes and its feathers are renewed in the scorching heat. The eagle then dips itself in a pool of water three times and becomes young again. So, believers are born into new life through baptism in the name of the Father, Son, and Holy Spirit.[295]

St. Mary: Towards the central middle portion of the façade is the image of Mother of God or St. Mary enthroned; is another

[293] Ibid., 19.

[294] Ibid., 99; Ezek. 1:4-10; 10:14; Rev. 4:6-7.

[295] Ibid., 99.

representation of Mary where she is seated on a throne holding the infant Jesus on her lap; represents that she is the *Theotokos.*[296]

Angels: Next to it we find four angels in either side blowing trumpets. The trumpet is used symbolically as a signal of alarm or triumph.[297] This may be the source of the use of trumpet as a verb, meaning "to spread good news." Christian depictions of the Last Judgement show angels blowing trumpets to announce the end of the world.[298]

Fish: The earliest literary reference to the fish as Christian symbol was made by Clement of Alexandria, who advised Christians to use a dove or fish as their seal. The fish, ever-watchful with its unblinking eyes, was one of the most important symbols of Christ to the early Christians. In Greek, the phrase, "Jesus Christ, Son of God Savior," is "*Iesous Christos Theou Yios Soter.*" The first letters of each of these Greek words, when put together, spell "*ichthys*," the Greek word for "fish" (*ICQUS*).[299] This symbol can be seen in the Sacraments Chapel of the Catacombs of St. Callistus. Because of the story of the miracle of the loaves and fishes, the fish symbolized, too, the Eucharist. In the early years of the church, believers called themselves sons of the celestial Ichthus. In the second century, Tertullian wrote, "We small fish like our Fish, Jesus Christ, swim in the (baptismal) water, and we can be saved only by remaining in it". In the third century, Cyprian wrote, "it is in the water that we are reborn, in the likeness of Christ or Master, the Fish." The fish became a common sign used by persecuted Christians to identify themselves as believers- a secret sign of faith.[300]

Lamb: Is the symbol of Christ as the Paschal Lamb and also a symbol for Christians (as Christ is our Shepherd and Peter was told

---

[296] Theotokos-from Greek Theos, meaning "God", and *tikto* meaning "to give birth to". The title was bestowed on the Virgin Mary by the Council of Ephesus in AD 431.

[297] Isa. 27:13; Ezek. 33:3; Joel 2:1; Zech. 9:14; Matt. 6:2; 1 Corin. 15:52; 1 Thess. 4:16; Rev. 1:10.

[298] Ibid., 125.

[299] https://www.fisheaters.com/symbols.html (02 Mar. 2017).

[300] Ibid.

to feed His sheep). The lamb is also a symbol for St. Agnes virgin martyr of the early Church. Christ is the Lamb of God, who takes away the sin of the world.[301] The lamb is the principal element in several representational variations with other elements- it is shown with a cross, with a cruciform halo, with blood flowing into a chalice, and with the banner of the Resurrection.[302]

Steps: The church building is almost at the same level as that of the ground but is raised 1 feet above the ground level which is a negligible height as far as building construction is concerned. As such, there are only few steps to enter the church proper near each *poomukham.*

Granite Cross: A long granite cross about fifteen feet in height is erected at the west side ofthe church. But this cross is a newly erected one. It is believed that there was an old cross at the north side earlier, which was removed for some reasons which is unknown.[303]

Interior Features

1. *Madbaha*: The position of the *madbaha* is raised, as it is in other churches. The width of them adbaha span about ten feet. There are seven steps from the Holy place to the *dargo* (step) of the altar. The sanctuary is rectangular shaped with a semi-circular vault made of laterite in the form of ornate niches. We find one *thronos* (altar) at the sanctuary which is devoid of any ornamentation. But earlier there was an ornate board on the altar which was removed. There are only few windows which are very small in size, and lets only very little light inside.

In Syrian Churches, the *madbaha* is the most elevated space of the edifice. The planes gradually ascend from the exterior to the sanctum sanctorum. Due to the reverence attached to odd numbers in the Eastern tradition, the total number of steps leading to the *madbaha* and the number of steps rising from the *qestromo* to the

---

[301] Isa. 53:6,7; John 1:29;1 Peter 1:19; Rev. 5:6

[302] Alva William Steffler, *Symbols of the Christian Faith* (Grand Rapid, Michigan: William B. Eerdmans Publishing Company, 2002), 9.

[303] Ibid., 12.

madbaha are usually odd in number. However, after the coming of the Portuguese we do not see any attachment to odd numbers.[304]

Signs and Symbols Concerning *Madbaha:* Steps rising up to the *mabbaha* represents the steps to salvation and the steps to heaven that Jacob, son of Isaac, dreamt of. The arch of the *madbaha* represents the union of heaven and earth when Jesus took the human form. The sanctuary is separated from the congregation by the veil or curtain (*Syr. Parokhet*) signifying the skies separating the heavens from the earth. *Madbaha* or the sanctum sanctorum signifies the union of God and mankind.[305]

So many steps leads to the church, in the case of a church built at a height, and inside the church further there are stepping stones to ascend to the holy place and the holy of the Holies. The *dargo, syr.* (Meaning step) adjacent to the altar, also has a meaning (the ascend and descend of the priest) - signifies the angels ascending and descending the ladder to heaven in Patriarch Jacob's dream.[306] This also means a spiritual ascent or spiritual growth attained through Christian life. Another example is the ascent of Moses to the summit of Mount Sinai for receiving the covenant from Yahweh;[307] indicates a mystical ascent towards God and spiritual austerity.

In a Hindu temple, the deity resides within a small dark *Girbhagrha* and the transitory spaces are organised in order of increasing sacredness to the final point of arrival in front of the divine power. This system of drawing the devotee to the sanctuary through a mysterious, dark space which culminates at the *madbaha*, lit by lamps and candles, incensed by censer, filled with the chimes of bells is very notable in old churches.[308]

The raised sanctuary represents the position of the heaven above and its glory. The *madbaha* has one altar and is surmounted by an intricately carved vault made of laterite stone with decorated

---

304 Op Cit., 11.

305 Ibid., 13.

306 Thomas Mar Athanasius, ed., *Nazrani Devalaya Vasthuvidya* (Kottayam: MOC Publications, 2007), 18.

307 Exo. 19-20.

308 Thomas Mar Athanasius, *Nazrani Devalaya Vasthuvidya*........... 35.

niches.[309] The vault of the sanctuary indicates the vault of heaven and its glory and awe.[310] In the case of Kallooppara church, the sanctuary is approached from the *hykala* by a flight of seven stone steps upto the *dargo* (syr. Meaning step of the *Thronos or altar*). Numbers are used frequently in the Bible (especially in prophetic and apocalyptic works) and in Christian pictorial symbols to signify various theological concepts. Seven is the number of perfection. God rested on the seventh day. Paul lists seven gifts of the Spirit and Jesus spoke seven utterances from the cross. The number seven is especially prominent in the apocalyptic Book of Revelation, in which there are seven seals, seven churches and many other things numbering seven.[311] Also in biblical numerology, seven is the most significant of sacred numbers. It is the number of completeness, fullness and perfection. In medieval Europe there was a predilection for establishing series of seven- the seven virtues, the seven arts and sciences, the seven sacraments, the seven ages of man and the seven deadly sins.[312]

2. *Thronos*: Is located at distance of 1.2m from the east wall of the madbaha. This space is ample and optimum for circumambulation.[313]Another two altars are placed at the *kestromo*, which are slightly smaller than the main altar at the *madbaha*. Surmounting these two altars are two canopies or *Kudish Kudishin*[314] which are ornate and beautiful adorned with colours.

Signs and Symbols Concerning *Thronos*: The altar (*thronos*-Syr.) is the throne of the HolyTrinity, and the altar canopy is the expressive symbol of is awe and majesty. Three forms of canopies are popular. They are:

a) Ciborium or Ciborium magnum(Gr.)
b) Baldachin(Syr.)
c) Tester

---

[309] Niche- a shallow recess, especially one in a wall to display a statue or other ornament.

[310] Ps. 19:1

[311] http://www.religionfacts.com/number-symbols (24 Feb. 2017).

[312] Alva William Steffler, *Symbols of the Christian Faith*.............. 134.

[313] Circumambulation is the ceremonial procession around the altar or around the church during the time if liturgical offices.

[314] Kudish Kudishin -means Holy Of the Holies in Syriac.

The ciborium or ciborium magnum is a solid structure of metal, stone, marble, or wood, erected over the altar, supported on four or more columns, with a roof which is either domed, spherical or flat.[315] An example for such an altar canopy is found in the sanctuary of Karthikapally church, where the roof is flat shaped. Another beautiful canopy if found in the chapel of the Old seminary. There are depictions of angels, Eucharistic bread, chalice and ornate board in this canopy. All these ornate canopies and artefacts points out the glory of the sanctuary which is considered as the heaven, the abode of the Almighty.

The *baldachin* is a smaller and lighter structure in metal or wood or merely a light frame covered with silk. It is hung over the altar by chains attached to brackets fixed on the wall. The word *baldachinum* is derived from the Italian equivalent for Baghdad where the textile material made of silk, wool and metal thread warp used for the canopies was first made. This type of canopies are not found anywhere in Malankara churches.[316] The tester is a rectangular, square, round or conical shaped canopy made of rich fabric and stretched over a metal or wood frame, with a deep valence on the lower edge. The use of canopies became widespread in the 10th century C.E in Christian Church.[317]

Kudish Kudishin is solely the contribution of the West Syrian Church or the Syrian Orthodox church. The main proof is its name itself, which is in Western Syriac. Secondly the evidence that the use of *Kudish Kudishin* was common in Syrian Orthodox church is from the narration of St. Gregorios of *Parumala*[318] who saw this in Syrian Orthodox churches in the Holy Land, on his visit there in 1895.

---

[315] Fr. K Mani Rajan, *Queen of Sacraments: A Treatise on the Liturgy of the Holy Mass Celebrated in the Syrian Orthodox Church* (Mulanthuruthy: Seminary Publications, 1994), 26.

[316] Ibid., 26.

[317] Ibid., 26.

[318] Saint Geevargese Mar Gregorios popularly known as Parumala Thirumeni (Bishop of Parumala) (15 June 1848 – 2 November 1902) was a bishop of the Malankara Orthodox Syrian Church. He is also known as Chathuruthil Kochu Thirumeni. He is the first canonized Christian saint from India and of the Malankara Orthodox Church.

In short *Kudish Kudishin* means a sanctuary inside a sanctuary; a small wooden *madbaha* inside a *madbaha.*[319]All these adds to the importance and glory of the sanctuary because it represents heaven, the dwelling place of God.

3. Arch: Arch or vault of the *madbaha* spans over the width and is beautifully ornate and is adorned with cornices and drops. The arch correspond to the vault of heaven and reaches the top most portion of the roof at the *kestromo.*

Signs and Symbols Concerning Arch: In all of Eastern Orthodox churches and Churches in Syrian tradition, there is widespread use of arches which are semi-circular in shape unlike the Gothic arches in Western tradition. Provision of such arches have got a deep meaning and theology. The front of the sanctuary (*madbaha*), in churches of Syrian tradition is decorated by an arch. The incarnation of our Lord unites together the Heaven and earth is the theological implication behind this provision. The historical truths from the Nativity of our Lord to His second coming is celebrated through worship in the holy *madbaha* and each faithful partakes in these great incarnational mysteries. The incarnational mysteries are guarded by the pillars of faith, which is represented by the pillars holding the arch of the Sanctuary.[320]

4. *Kestromo*: The *kestromo* until recent times had tall wooden architraves[321] at the position of railings and an arch at the centre. But this was demolished in a later period, the date of which is

[319] Thomas Mar Athanasius, ed., *Nazrani Devalaya Vasthuvidya* (Kottayam: MOC Publications, 2007), 47.

[320] Ibid., 17.

[321] An architrave : architrave "chief beam", also called an epistyle; from Greek ἐπίστυλον epistylon "door frame") is the lintel or beam that rests on the capitals of the columns. It is an architectural element in Classical architecture. The term can also be applied to all sides, including the vertical members, of a frame with mouldings around a door or window. The word architrave is also used to refer more generally to a style of mouldings (or other elements) framing the top of a door, window or other rectangular opening, where the horizontal "head" casing extends across the tops of the vertical side casings where the elements join.

unknown.[322] Two small altars occupy the south and north side of the *kestromo* which are on raised platforms. Although, there are no ornamental canopies a simple board surmounts the altars with an architrave at west side which are made of wood which are intricately painted; and this seems to be a recent addition. On the topmost part outside the arch of the *madbaha* we find a cross with leaves at its bottom which is a rare symbol in churches. There is another solid evidence of the antiquity of the church. The granite slab at the *kestromo* has ancient inscription in local *Vattezhuthu* (Old Dravidian dialect) script regarding when the church was built. This is probably one of the early centuries of the last millennium, according to the many archaeological inferences.[323]

5. *Hykala*: The *hykala* was much short in earlier times. During the 1970's the western side was extended and the length of the *hykala* was increased. The construction was with concrete, with beams and columns to connect with the existing portion. A new façade was also erected at the west side with the existing old façade on the extreme west side. Renovation of the extended portion started in 1997 and the work was completed in 2008. At the western side of the *hykala*, inside the church is a balcony made of wood. In earlier times there was a resting room for the clergy.

6. Doors and Windows: Mainly there is the main door at the western side of the church and the door is made of wood and ornate with metal studs. The other doors are present at the northern and southern side of the church. Apart from this we observe two doors each at these portions which are later additions done during renovation. Like any other ancient churches in Kerala, in this church too we don't find any window inside the church, at the nave portion. But we find a couple of small door like windows measuring 1m x 0.80m at either side of the *madbaha*.

Signs and Symbols Concerning Doors and Windows: Windows were not provided inside the *hykala* or inside the *madbaha*.

---

322 Fr. C. K. Kurien, ed., *Kallooppara Valiya Palli- Sahashrabda Smaranika* (Thiruvalla: St. Mary's Church Publication, 2001), 37.

323 Ibid., 36.

Introduction of windows happened only after the advent of the Portuguese. The Synod of Diamper insisted windows for the *madbaha*; a small window was introduced above the height of the celebrant and these were not sufficient to let in light. Inspite of the Latinization efforts in church architecture, the mystery element to be maintained of the Holy Eucharist, which is part and parcel of Eastern Mysticism, was never overthrown in *Nazrani*[324] churches.[325] In some other old churches, adjacent to the wall of the altar we find circular openings.[326] A full circle symbolises eternity. This represents a symbol, of worship, which leads us to eternal life.[327]

Acoustics is another important concern inside the church building. One of the best examples for good acoustic design in Kerala, is the Chapel at the Old Seminary, Kottayam. The acoustics inside the seminary chapel gives us a feeling of joy and spiritual enlightenment. It helps us create an atmosphere conducive for worship. The semi-circular door and the arch shaped false roof with decorative niches aids in proper acoustics in and around the sanctuary. This in turn avoids reverberation and echo effects which makes worship audible, lively and divine.[328]

7. Ornamentations: We see ornamental works on wooden beams, doors and at the cloisters of the veranda near to the nave portion which are intricate and corresponds to *vastu* principles. These art works brings out the true art forms in wood by the artisans of Kerala in olden days. These were introduced so as to increase the aesthetics of the interiors of the church. Other fine ornamental

---

[324] Nazrani- The Saint Thomas Christians or Thomas Christians, also called Syrian Christians or Nasrani, are a community of Christians from Kerala, India, who trace their origins to the evangelistic activity of Thomas the Apostle in the 1st century.

[325] Ibid., 18.

[326] In 1876, on the arrival of H.H. Peter III, he insisted to provide three slits with stained glass on the eastern wall of the sanctuary. According to the Patriarch this represented the Holy Trinity. As a result of this we see this arrangement provided in all the churches which was built during this period.

[327] Ibid., 19.

[328] Thomas Mar Athanasius, ed., *Nazrani Devalaya Vasthuvidya* (Kottayam: MOC Publications, 2007), 18.

works are found in the *malika muri* (rest room) situated at the first floor level of the veranda. The presence of ornamentations and elements like *deepasthambams* (stone graded wick lamps) and stone lamps (*chirathu*-Malayalam) along the compound walls bears close resemblance to Hindu temples.

Signs and Symbols Concerning Ornamentation: There is another striking symbol of a cross which is adorned with leaves below, at the top of the vault of the sanctuary. The leaves represents the leaves of the tree of life. It is a clear representation of the cross of Golgotha, with the tree of life, the cross in Paradise, i.e., Golgotha. Similar such cross is found in a tomb at Ma'in in Jordan and dated back to 7th century A.D.[329] The symbolism of cross and its theology is mentioned in the architecture of Kaduthuruthy church.

8. Bas-Relief: Even though, we find numerous reliefs outside the church, it is few inside. The most striking one is the cross with leaves at the base, at the top most part of the *kestromo* above the arch of the sanctuary.

9. Baptismal Font: The baptismal font is placed at the south east portion of the nave. It is madeout of granite and looks considerably old without any reliefs.

St. Mary's Knanaya Catholic Church, Kaduthuruthy

Historical Background

Kaduthuruthy Valiya Palli of *Knanaya*[330] Community is a historic church, originally established in AD 400. Located in Kaduthuruthy, the present Kaduthuruthy St. Mary's Valiya Palli is a third building serving the congregation, and is linked to the history of the *Knanaya* community known as Southists. Kaduthuruthy Valiya Palli had a glorious history in the past with its supreme position with the Vadakkumkur (present Vaikom in Kerala) Kingdom. The first church

---

[329] Joseph Vazhuthanpally, *The Biblical and Archaeological Foundations of the Mar Thoma Sliba*………… 28.

[330] The *Knanaya*, also known as the Southists or *Tekkumbhagar*, are an endogamous group in the Saint Thomas Christian community of Kerala, India. They are differentiated from another part of the community, known in this context as the Northists.

was called *chathura* pally meaning Square shaped church.[331] The history of this church is manifested with the history of the *Knanaya* community or the Jewish Christians known as Southist Syrian Christians now a day's termed as *Knanites.* The present building is the third building in Kaduthuruthy constructed in AD 1456 and it had a strong fort as mentioned in the song of the church. Thus, the present church building is constructed with all its artistic splendour and characteristics of Gothic Art, to proclaim and celebrate the gospel of Jesus Christ in worship and value the heritage of biblical faith, tradition, liturgy and the rich variety of customs and tradition in *Knanaya* Community guided by the forefathers. This church belongs to the Archdiocese of Kottayam and is considered as the Head Church for both *knanaya* Catholics and *Knanaya* Jacobites.[332]

Architecture of Kaduthuruthy Church

Exterior Features

1. Roof: The roof is gabled one but is situated at a much higher level than the other two churches. This is due to the walls being at a higher level. The gable incorporates purlins and rafters followed by tiled roofing which is put up according to *vastu shastra* principles as detailed in the architecture of Kallooppara church.

2. *Poomukham*: There is a *poomukham* on the north side of the church and a door opening. This door is called the *'anavathil'* or the big door and is the main entrance to the church. The *poomukham* is built according to *vastu* principles. A plinth beam like short wall encircles the *poomukham.* Details about *poomukham* is mentioned in the Kallooppara church architecture.

Signs and Symbols Concerning *Poomukham:* On observation of the exterior wall, at the northern and western door jambs we find the images of two *makaras*[333] on either side. They are the *dwarapalas,*

---

[331] Fr. Mathew Cherusseril, *Kadathuruthy Valiapally* (Kottayam: The Catholic Mission Press Training Centre, 1982), 26.

[332] https://en.wikipedia.org/wiki/Kaduthuruthy_Valiya_Palli (24 Feb. 2017).

[333] Makara-is a sea-creature in Hindu culture. It is generally depicted as half terrestrial animal in the frontal part (stag, deer, crocodile, or elephant) and half aquatic animal in the hind part (usually a fish or seal tail, though sometimes a peacock or

who are always watchful in their duty in guarding the door of the house of God.

3. Front Elevation or Façade: The front façade of the church is one of the beautiful facades in the ancient churches of Kerala. There are numerous bas-reliefs which are beautifully preserved to this day. It is evident that this façade was built after the advent of the Portuguese. On inspection of the west side façade we observe many symbols.

Signs and Symbols Concerning Façade

Angel: An angel holding a balance stamping the devil indicates the final judgement which forall who are born to the earth.

Lion: On either side of the façade at the middle are two lions. The lion is one of Christ's messianic titles.[334] Like the eagle, the lion represents royal dominion. The lion also symbolizes strength and courage, and thus was adopted as the insignia of the Roman legions around the time of Christ. In addition, the lion represents justice because of the biblical description of Solomon's throne of Justice, which rested on six steps guarded by twelve magnificent lions.[335]

Saints: There are images of St. Mary, St. Paul and St. Peter. On the topmost end, just below the cross we see the image of St. Mary being crowned by the Holy Trinity, signifies that eternal crown shall be given to all who are righteous like St. Mary, where all the three Godheads are represented symbolically.

Image of Man and Woman with Mermaid Body: The image of a man and woman with a fish tail holding a ship represents the spiritual dimension of the advent of the *Knanaites* to Kerala in AD

---

even a floral tail is depicted. Makara take many different forms throughout Asia. In Hindu astrology, Makara is equivalent to the sign of Capricorn, tenth of the twelve symbols of the Zodiac. Makara appears as the vahana (vehicle) of the river goddess Ganga and of the sea god Varuna. Makara are considered guardians of gateways and thresholds, protecting throne rooms as well as entryways to temples; it is the most commonly recurring creature in Hindu and Buddhist temple iconography, and also frequently appears as a Gargoyle or as a spout attached to a natural spring.

[334] Gen. 49:9; Rev. 5:5.

[335] Alva William Steffler, *Symbols of the Christian Faith*............ 15: 1 Kings 10: 18-20.

345 through the sea in a ship. Other notable symbols are the niches which are triangular, rectangular and square shaped.[336]

Peacock: Another image is the peacock. Peacock is a symbol of immortality (even St. Augustine believed the peacock's flesh to have "antiseptic qualities" and that it didn't corrupt), the peacock became a symbol of Christ and the Resurrection. It is also seen as an appropriate symbol of the promise that will be raised "incorruptible."[337] Its image embellished everything from the Catacombs to everyday objects, like lamps, especially in early Romanesque and Byzantine churches. (The peacock, for obvious reasons, was also used as a symbol for pride, too).[338]

Hunter, Deer, Leopard and Dog: On the east side wall at the top, just below the roof we find bas relief of a hunter, dog, deer and leopard. This is a very meaningful symbolism. Leopard is connected with antichrist by some. By association, the leopard is a symbol of sin and the great destroyer, Satan. The image of the hunter indicates the destruction of the evil or Satan by Divine intervention. The deer

---

[336]The square is a symbol of the earth, in contrast to the circle, which represents the heavens. In design it is the most static, no-dynamic of shapes and is therefore used to suggest balance and resolution.

As part of the system of 'sacred geometry and proportion' in the tradition of icon production, the rectangle, based on the ratio of 4:3, is considered the geometrical symbol of harmony. Christian artists have related the proportional relationship of the Golden Section to the mystery of God; for this reason it is called the Divine proportion.

In the early years of Christianity, the Manicheans (Manichaeism taught an elaborate dualistic cosmology describing the struggle between a good, spiritual world of light, and an evil, material world of darkness. Through an ongoing process which takes place in human history, light is gradually removed from the world of matter and returned to the world of light, whence it came. Its beliefs were based on local Mesopotamian gnostic and religious movements) used the triangle as a symbol of the Trinity, which led Augustine to reject its use. Nevertheless, it ultimately prevailed as a shape that represents the Trinity (Alva William Steffler, *Symbols of the Christian Faith*........ 80-81).

[337] I Corin. 15:52

[338] Alva William Steffler, *Symbols of the Christian Faith*........... 30.

represents the ordinary man who is susceptible to the evil. The image of the dog indicates watchfulness of Christian life.[339]

4. Ornate Columns: The *poomukham* is supported by means of four columns made of granite with minimal ornamentation but has got bas-reliefs of certain animals like deer, elephant, etc. These columns takes up the load of the *poomukham* and is scientifically designed in accordance to *vastu shastra.*

5. Steps: as the entrance or the *poomukham* is not raised much from the growing level, the number of steps also are few. The few steps are made out of granite pieces cut in shape to suit the *poomukham* plinth dimension. Details about step is mentioned in the architecture of Thiruvithamcode church.

6. Granite Cross: The huge stone cross installed at the Eastern side of the Kaduthuruthy church is 40 feet tall and this is considered as the tallest stone cross in Kerala.[340] The base is 10 feet in long, 10 feet wide and 10 feet high. There are bas-reliefs of lion, elephant, leopard, pig, deer, camel, cock and several varieties of floral arrangement. All these adds to the aesthetic beauty of the cross.

Interior Features

1. *Madbaha:* The roof of the *madbaha* is a semicircular vault made of laterite stone and has intricately adorned niches. The entrance to the madbaha is 12 foot long. The altar is situated at the centre of the *madbaha* and is surmounted by a beautifully ornate wooden canopy with images flowers and fruits. These works are attributed to the 16th century.[341] The size of the sanctuary is smaller, especially the breadth, than the *Kestromo* and is heavily decorated.

2. *Thronos*: There are images of St. Mary, St. Peter and St. Paul at the altar and behind it onto a wooden board fitted at the east wall. There is also the relief of Pelican bird under the altar. The sanctuary has at its entrance the vault which has ornate niches intricately designed. The sanctuary like other ancient churches in Kerala is raised. The

339 Ibid., 114.

340 Fr. Mathew Cherusseril, *Kaduthuruthy Valiya Palli* .... 49.

341 Fr. Mathew Cherusseril, *Kaduthuruthy Valiya Palli* .... 50.

vault and the roof above it is slightly raised than the roof of the *Hykala and Kestromo.*

Signs and Symbols in *Thronos*: On the altar front there is the image of the pelican. The Pelican is a symbol of the atonement and the Redeemer and is often found in Christian murals, frescos, paintings and stained glass. The pelican was believed to wound itself in order to feed its young with its own blood. St. Thomas Aquinas addresses the Saviour as, "Pelican of Mercy.'[342]

3. Arch: As in Kallooppara church, the arch or the vault of the *madbaha* is ornate with aesthetic designs and with coloured niches. Other details and symbolism is mentioned in the architecture of Kallooppara church.

4. *Kestromo:* The *kestromo* has on is northern and southern side two ornate canopies with the statues of St. Mary and St. Sebastian. There are no altars at the *kestromo* area but the area below the canopies resembles an altar space. Details and symbolism concerning canopies are mentioned in the architecture of Kallooppara church.

5. *Hykala:* The *hykala* extends from the *kestromo* to the west end. There is a balcony on the western side made out of wood.

6. Doors and Windows: The main entrance is at the northern side which leads to the *poomukham.* At the west side there is a door which is small in size, but made out of wood and beautifully studded with brass. There are other doors at the southern and north western parts of the church. Other details concerning door are mentioned in the architecture of Kallooppara church and Thiruvithamcode church.

There are no windows inside the church in the old structure. In the *hykala* portion and doors are at the west, north and south sides. The absence of windows inside the church shows that the structure was built before the advent of Portuguese. Few windows present are later additions. The walls of the church 3 foot thick. This is a structural adaptation at the same time provides comfort for those inside the church. The huge walls are filled with sand, so as to provide a heat

[342] Alva William Steffler, *Symbols of the Christian Faith*.............. 37.

insulation which aids in providing a cool atmosphere inside the church.

7. Ornamentations: One of the most important feature of this church is the presence of threetypes of crosses at different walls of the structure:

1. Parakum Cross or Winged cross (Sliba[343]): means that the sliba has wings and it can fly. The sliba is compared to a bird and says that the sliba came like a bird flying.
2. Persian Cross: It is found on the open air granite base on which the cross is erected. It is dated back to the 8th century A.D.
3. Mountain Cross: This is a granite cross found from a tomb stone. The inscription is the dedication to a man at rest in the tomb. It is dated back to the 14h Century.

Signs and Symbols of Ornamentations: The cross of Jesus Christ is central to the Christian faith. The cross reveals to us the character of God: His love for lost sinners and His perfect justice meet at the cross. Joseph Vazhuthanaally opines that the real foundation for any theological symbol especially the cross rests on the Biblical testimony, Patrological interpretation, liturgical evidence and archaeological excavation and the use of that in the Holy Church. Accordingly, certain signs or pictographical figures or material objects can signify and symbolize the cross. Hebrew letter "Taw" is a symbol of the cross. Origen wanted to explore and make sure of the significance of the letter 'taw' and recognized it as the cross.[344]

As quoted by Joseph Vazhuthanapally, Mar Aphrem, the Syrian Father, says:

---

[343] Sleeba or Sliba is the Aramaic word meaning "cross". The traditional Nazarani sleeba is quite old, and comes from a scan of a Daqin cross found in Xi'an, China, which was a major centre of Christian life during the first millinium A.D. Other examples of similar crosses have been found everywhere from Sri Lanka to Siberia and Japan to eastern Turkey, carved into Nazarani buildings, in cave art, on icons and on a number of pieces of pottery, grave stones and other artefacts.

[344] Joseph Vazhuthanpally, *The Biblical and Archaeological Foundations of the Mar Thoma Sliba*............ 30.

Only Jesus has perfected the symbols of the Scriptures through His Cross, its types in His body, the jewels in its beauty.

The primitive Christian community and the apostolic holy Fathers in the light of Jesus' mission, life, death and resurrection tried to trace out the prefiguration, typologies and symbols of the cross from the Old Testament from the very early days of Christian era. The holy Fathers looked at the cross from an angle of faith and prayer and saw it as the fulfilment of the eternal plan of God in the Scriptures and the prophecies. Some of the symbols of the cross in the Old Testament are: the tree of life of the paradise, the ark of Noah, Jacob's ladder, the raised arms of Moses, the bronze serpent.[345]

There are approximately four hundred variations on the basic shape of the cross. Latin cross, Greek cross, Advent cross, Patriarchal cross, Eastern Orthodox cross, Celtic cross, Graded cross and budded cross are some of the common types. As far as the St. Thomas Christians[346] are considered the Marthoman Sleeba[347] is of much importance. The cross is seen as a sign of complete resolution between the vertical life force and the horizontal death or 'rest' force. Perhaps most importantly, it represents life's polarities: the spiritual or other worldly (vertical) and the physical or worldly (horizontal).

---

[345] Ibid., 31.

[346] The St. Thomas Christians are the most ancient Christians of Malabar, the south west coast of India. Some affirm the origin of the Thomas Christians from the preaching of the Apostle St. Thomas. The oldest written account that speaks of the labours of St. Thomas in India is the work known as the Acts of Judas Thomas written most probably in Syriac in the second or third century. (Placid J. Podippara, The Thomas Christians……15).

[347] Marthoma Sliba was discovered from Great Mount of Mailapur, Tamil Nadu. In 1547 while the Portuguese Jesuits were digging the foundations of the church on the Great mount of Mailapur they found a stone slab with a cross sculptured upon it and an inscription running round the edge of the cross. There was also the Biblical verse from the Syriac Peshitta- Gal. 6:14- in a hand writing which is olde than 10th century. After this epoch-making event of the discovery of Marthoma Sliba soon there were found many such similar crosses from Alangad, Changanassery, Kadamattam, Kaduthuruthy, Kothanellur, Kottayam, Kuravilangad etc. (Joseph Vazhuthanapally, The Biblical and Archaeological Foundations of the Mar Thoma Sliba ……………….. 8-9).

Mar Aphrem, the Syrian father, is very clear about the concept of the cross-tree, the fruits of the cross and the fruits of the tree. The cross of Jesus was made of wood and in the primitive time the altar too was of wood in order to have an association with the tree, wood and the cross off Jesus. "Jesus came from the heavenly height/place, Jesus has ascended to the height of the cross: so that the cross would replace the tree; Adam had deprived of its glory, instead of the fruit of the tree, you have the fruit of the cross, who is the crucified Jesus."

8. Bas-relief: On the eastern side of the altar we find bas-reliefs of the wonderful scene of St. Mary being gloriously received at heaven and with the great company of apostles, saints and hosts of angels with all musical instruments the Holy Trinity- the Father, Son and the Holy Spirit adorned as three persons, giving the crown of heaven.[348] Below this are the reliefs of St. Peter and St. Paul who are the chief of the apostles. This arrangement made in ornamental wood panel is called Rathol popularly known as *'erathazhu*[349] in Malayalam.

9. Baptismal Font: On the southern side is the baptistery with a very old baptismal font[350] made out of granite with bas-reliefs of St. Mary with infant Jesus and images of John the Baptist baptising Jesus.

Common Features of these Churches

1. Roof: For all the three structures the roof is gabled with purlins and rafters and atop the tileis laid. This conforms to *vastu shastra* principles. This also show the adaptation done for the churches to take care of the atmospheric condition- as Kerala gets plenty rainfall throughout the year and hence drainage at roof top if important. Gabled roof caters to this need,

2. *Poomukham*: Is found in all the three cases and is built according to *vastu vidya*. This show that it is an indispensable part of ancient Christian churches in Kerala.

---

[348] Fr. Mathew Cherusseril, *Kaduthuruthy Valiya Palli* .... 49.

[349] Erathazhu was introduced in the Kerala churches during the Portuguese period and remained in Nazrani churches even after the Oath of Koonen Cross.

[350] The baptismal font made of rock at Kaduthururthy church is the biggest one in Kerala.

3. *Madbaha:* conforms to a common plan even though the dimensions vary. The use of semi-circular arch or vault at the entrance and for the ceiling of the *madbaha* is same for Kallooppara church and Kaduthuruthy churches.

4. Front Elevation: in all the three cases the façade has so many features in common; this was a development after the advent of the Portuguese.

5. Baptismal Font: in all the churches it is made of granite and has some ornamentations.

Summary

This chapter was intended to study about the theological aspects of certain signs and symbols used in Christian church and also the theological elements prevalent in the architecture of ancient churches of Kerala with special emphasis on three churches which were selected for the case study namely Thiruvthamcode St. Mary's church, Kallooppara St. Mary's church and Kaduthuruthy St. Mary's church. It also covers the structural and spatial organisation of the ancient church building in Kerala and its theological implications.

On primary observation we see that all the three churches have certain commonalities, especially in the basic plan- the position and size of the *madbaha* when compared to the *kestromo and hykala*. The sanctuary in all the three cases has its width less than the *kestromo.* The roof of the sanctuary, except in Thiruvithamcode church, is a semicircular vault (Thiruvithamcode church was built in the 6th century and during that time there was no fixed principles and criteria for church architecture in South India) which is ornate in both the other churches; points to the common principle that the roof should be semi-circular as it represents the glory of the heaven. In all the three cases we observe certain principles and proportion for the structure which is none other than *vastu* principles which was prevalent in temple architecture. The construction of *poomukhams* and their ornate cloisters and the gabled system of roofing is the best example. The artisans were the local Hindus and their workmanship definitely involved the use of *vastu sastra.* In short we can infer that the *vastu shastra* and *thachu shastra* formed the part and parcel of not only Hindu temples and other domestic building but also Christian churches of Kerala.

Along with this we also observe, in all the three cases, the widespread use of signs and symbols which communicates to a great extent the faith and theology of the Christian community in Kerala or the St. Thomas Christians. But in the indigenous church architecture we find the influences of the East Syrian Church, Roman Catholic Church and West Syrian Church architecture. Hence, we can talk about a blended form of Church architecture in Kerala and that itself makes it a unique form of Religious architecture.

Towards an Indigenous Church Architecture

The most important concern regarding church architecture is the utility factor. The church building should pertain to the worship needs of a particular congregation. Very often large edifices are put up as worship places for a small parish with less number of parishioners. Tens of thousands and crores of money is being spent for these huge structures, which cannot be justified in a Christian point of view. When constructing a church building, it should be noted that the structure should cater to the worshipful needs of the parish. Maximum utility should be made available for the purpose of worship rather than the believers' comfort

Today the trend among the Syrian Christians of Kerala is to build huge church structures. No planning and care is taken for the proper maintenance of such gigantic structures. An indigenous form of architecture should be envisaged, taking into account the local *thachu shastra and vastu vidya* principles, and at the same time the structure need to be constructed according to latest engineering and structural technology. In all other Eastern Orthodox churches, both in Byzantine and Oriental Orthodox churches, it is a matter of concern to have a uniform pattern and architectural aesthetics when constructing a church building. The Indian Orthodox church has no such criteria, which is a drawback, when considering the identity of the Syrian Christians.

It has become a common practice to use different types of arches in the newly built churches. The common among them is the Gothic arch. Gothic arches made its way into the local church architecture of Kerala, as a result of the influence of the Portuguese. Gothic, Romanesque and Baroque architectural traditions are predominantly Catholic in nature. Nowhere, in Orthodox architecture have we seen Gothic arches. In Orthodox architectural tradition only semi-circular arches are used, which in turn has got a theological significance, which the former lacks. This is not a matter of major concern for the new church builders. Orthodox architecture and theology is equally important as liturgy and worship, hence it should not be neglected and should not be according to the whims and fancies of some individuals.

Another notable feature is the presence of doors and windows inside the church building. Windows were not provided insidethe *hykala* or inside the *madbaha.* Introduction of windows happened only after the advent of the Portuguese. After the cement concrete revolution in India, the introduction of new cement concrete structures paved way for new engineering techniques and concepts, especially regarding doors and windows. Buildings were built to be more airy and allowing maximum light, which led to the placement of more number of windows and doors. This was introduced in church buildings too. An introspection into the structure and arrangement of windows and doors in churches built a century ago and before, reveals certain important facts. There were no windows at all inside the church building. Small openings or ventilators were provided, on either sides, above the lintel level for cross ventilation. The lighting inside the church was reduced to the minimum; usually a semi-dark atmosphere prevailed even during daytime. This was intended to create a mystical experience inside the building. Darkness inside the church, unlike brightly lit interiors inside church buildings in the West, has got a strong theological basis in the Eastern churches. This is the reason why all the Eastern Orthodox churches adopts this principle for creating a mystical experience inside the spiritual edifice. The facts about 'divine darkness' is discussed in the third chapter, in detail. Another practical reason for the absence of windows is the need for proper acoustics. Clarity and amplification, to a little extent, was made available in old church structures very successfully. Nowadays, acoustics is not maintained inside the church building, even with the use of microphone.

When discussing about the presence of doors, the old churches possessed only three door, and this number did never change; which in turn has got a theological meaning. Today, in church buildings, maximum number of doors are provided which are intended merely to make the entry and exit easier; the theological significance is neglected. The theological connotation of the provision of doors is discussed in the third chapter. The provision of windows and doors inside a church building should be done with proper planning. This should be taken care of, when constructing new churches in future.

The new churches which were built after the second half of the twentieth century are not according to any particular dimensions. This is a drawback in church construction. There is a certain proportion regarding the height or the head room and the width of the nave portion. The height and the width of the nave portion need to be equal in dimension. This thumb rule is very important, as this thumb rule is the decisive factor in proper acoustics inside the nave of the church. In many of the newly constructed churches' this is not followed, which leads to reverberation and echo of sound produced inside the church. Even the Canon (*Hudaya* Canon written by Bar Hebreaus in 13th CE; the Official Canon Accepted by the *Malankara* Orthodox Church) gives fixed rules and dimensions regarding the construction of altar and the sanctuary.

The position and size of the sanctuary is another important thing. The old churches exhibited sanctuaries which were small in area (Constricted *madbaha*), when compared to the width of the nave. The focus is towards the altar which is placed at the centre. The *madbaha* is raised and usually seven steps lead to the *dargo* (raised platform adjacent to the altar) of the *madbaha* from the nave. Number seven, biblically, has got a significance (Seven represents perfectness and wholeness). Biblical numerology has importance in architectural theology too. The ceiling (false ceiling) of the sanctuary is a semi-circular vault. This aids in good acoustics inside the church building. The main ceiling above the semi-circular vaulted ceiling is at a higher level than the roof of the nave portion, the theological importance of which is enlisted in the third chapter. The sanctuary is void of windows in most cases; minimal light is provided inside the *madbaha*. This has similarity with the native Hindu *sreekovil* or sanctuary, where bright light is totally restricted. In both cases the darkness pertains to a mystical atmosphere. Today the sanctuaries are constructed with maximum width; width same as the width of the nave. We don't feel any mystical atmosphere and everything inside the sanctuary seem to be open to the congregation, even though the veil is present. It is a pity that none of these factors are taken into consideration in the construction of newly built churches.

Even though, Icons are not popular in the Syrian Orthodox church and Syrian Christian churches of Kerala, icons find a pivotal position in the religious life of Eastern Orthodox Christians. Icons are divine manifestations and not mere art forms and hence can speak volumes about the 'Divine'. It would be worth using these 'Divine images' in the churches of Kerala. Such an inculturation of religious art would be commendable. Mural paintings are the traditional paintings in Kerala. The colour used for painting is made out of vegetable and fruit juices and not enamel paints. These paintings are characteristics of Hindu temples and palatial mansions. Rarely mural paintings are found in ancient Christian churches too. One example is the painting at the eastern wall of the sanctuary of Cheppad St. George Orthodox church, Kerala. Another artefact is the'*erathazhu*, wooden screen depicting pictures of St. Mary and other saints, placed at the eastern wall of the sanctuary; present in *Mulanthuruthy Marthomman* Church (In Ernakulam District of Kerala). This indigenous form of art is worth acceptable. We need church buildings that would help in spiritual enlightening and creating a mystical experience conducive for worship rather than mere prayer halls.

The provision of secondary altar, even though not in Eastern tradition, has become a commonplace in Kerala centuries ago. This became part of Thomas Christian church architecture as a result of Latin Church influence. Today it is present in almost all the churches in *Malankara*. An important fact to be kept in mind is that these altars too should be given the same importance as that of the main altar and should be within a vaulted arch opening. The use of *Kudish Kudishin* (decorated wooden canopy) above the altar adds to the glory and aesthetics of the sanctuary, instead of the costly cladding of the sanctuary and nave walls with teakwood or rosewood. Never in the architecture of ancient churches have we seen the use of wooden cladded walls. These new trends cannot be entertained and such unnecessary expenses should be avoided.

One of best example for a church building of modern times built according to *vastu sastra* is St. John's Cathedral situated at Thiruvalla, Kerala. The *vastu silpa* involves the Keralite *thachu sastra* principles for its construction. This is evident from the interior and exterior view of the church. The columns have many things to communicate about the science of *vastu*, at the same time exhibits theological meanings which can influence human minds. The interesting feature of this edifice is that the *thachu shastra* principles are incorporated in contemporary fashion, elegantly and with aesthetic beauty. Another example is the newly built St Gregorios Chapel situated on the banks of river *Pamba at Maramon*, a town in the *Pathanamthitta* district of Kerala. The structure pertains to *vastu shastra* and *thachu shastra* princples built according to contemporary technology in an ancient and antique style.

To conclude, indigenous church architecture should help us to find the roots of ancient architectural tradition which a living entity, highlighting the faith and conviction of the Thomas Christian community which bears witness to the Life giving Gospels truths and messages of our Lord and Saviour Jesus Christ.

Conclusion

Church architecture has got volumes to communicate about the scripture and theology. This research intends to study about the theological elements in the architecture of selected ancient churches in Kerala on the basis of the scripture and the science of *vastu*. Gliding through the church architectures around the world, it could be manifested that the design of sacred places of worship has got indigenous influences which is evident in the *vastu shastra* of the selected churches in Kerala, for the study. The first chapter elaborates about the different types of church architecture around the world in different periods of time, starting from the early century to the present Post Modern time and its theological implications. The following chapter deals with the science of *vastu*, its principles and use in the construction of sacred spaces. The main crux of the study lies in the third chapter which includes the research of the indigenous architecture of the three churches, which stands as the representation of the architectural practices followed in the three important geographical regions of Kerala namely Thiruvithamcode St. Mary's church, Kallooppara St. Mary's church and Kaduthuruthy St. Mary's church. These three churches were selected on the basis of their locations. The first church is situated in the southern part of Kerala (now in Kanyakumari district of Tamil Nadu; this region was part of erstwhile Tranvancore before the formation of Kerala state). The second church, Kallooppara St. Mary's church is situated in the central Travancore and the third one Kaduthuruthy St. Mary's church is at northern Travancore. This selection based on location was intended for understanding the construction practices of churches and the theological elements involved in the architecture prevalent in different parts of Kerala in the ancient times, especially in the Pre-Portuguese period.

On detailed inspection and study of the three churches, it is observed that there are many similarities in church construction and architecture, at the same time there are a few variations too. These variations can be due to different reasons. One reason is the variations due to the involvement of different artisans or craftsmen, which can vary depending on person and place and their technical and artistic knowhow. Another reason is the availability of different construction materials, in plenty and their use, in different places. But we can infer that the basic plan and design for all churches, irrespective of place or artisans is the same.

The ecclesial relationship of the Thomas Christians with the East Syrian Church right from the early centuries brought about East Syrian elements, (One eg:- the use of semi-circular arches) in church architecture along with the liturgy. Until the advent of the Portuguese and the spread of Roman Catholic faith, the Church of St. Thomas was in close relation with the East Syrian Church. A solid evidence to substantiate this fact is the presence of Persian stone crosses in many of the ancient churches in Kerala.

By close observation and study it is also found that the Ancient Christian churches in Kerala have many commonalities with the Buddhist *chaitya grihas*, regarding the vaulted roof, the nave portion and the internal structure. In Jain temple architecture too we observe the presence of hallway and *mandapa* similar to that of Buddhist *chaityas.* This in turn has resemblance to Church architecture in Kerala during the ancient period. So, the Buddhist and Jain architecture also was influential, to a little extent, in the architecture of ancient churches.

The description of the architecture of ancient churches as model of Hindu temples points to the fact that these ancient churches were built according to *vastu* style. On the other end of the search for history, there was a science and style for the construction of sacred space intended for worship and this was necessary for creating an atmosphere conducive for worship. The age old *vastu silpas* and symbols bears witness to certain eternal truths concerning faith and conviction of the Christian community in Kerala. The advent of the Portuguese, brought about the cultural encroachment in Kerala and the helplessness of the local Christian community to safeguard their age old heritage and culture regarding church architecture, resulted in mere utility value church buildings in Kerala, thereafter.

Kerala had more than one hundred churches and a well-developed indigenous Church Architecture at the time of arrival of the Portuguese. The Portuguese and the missionaries who reached Kerala in the sixteenth century brought in Western ideas and ideologies of Church Architecture. They forcefully imposed Roman Catholicism and Latin liturgy in church of Kerala. Many new churches were built and the existing churches were remodelled in the sixteenth to seventeenth centuries. The new churches built during the sixteenth to seventeenth century exhibit an architectural character, which is different from the indigenous character of churches in Kerala. These churches possess an imposing front facade, ample light for the interior and a monumental character.

While all the churches established prior to 16th century are oriented in the East–West axis with the altar positioned in the East, the churches established after the advent of the Europeans, do not strictly follow this. The influence of the West on the church Architecture of Kerala is confirmed from this result. All the churches of the sixteenth and seventeenth centuries have an imposing front facade which is undoubtedly an imported element supplied to all the churches. A well-proportioned facade became the integral part of Kerala churches after the arrival of the Portuguese.

In short, the churches built before the advent of the Portuguese to Kerala, resembled Hindu temples and also was constructed according to *vastu* principles and *vastu shastra*. There are so many explanations to substantiate the fact about *vastu* influence in church architecture in the ancient churches in Kerala. The external architectural features of Hindu temples and Christian churches has so many similarities like the gabled roof system with *poomukhams* and columns with carvings. Examples for this is *Kallooppara* church and the nearby Devi temple. The one important thing that is different for Church and Temple is that the former has the cross at the top of the façade and the latter has the *shikara* at the top of the sanctuary. Temple *vastu* principles were followed for churches too, by the local Hindu artisans who built churches. This highlights the indigenous character of *Nazrani* churches which remained vibrant in its indegenity, in spite of Latin Church and also East and West Syrian Church influence in Kerala.

After the middle of the 17th century, after the Oath of *Koonen* Cross, the Thomas Christians came in ecclesial relation with the West Syrian Church or the Syrian Orthodox Church. This again was influential as far as church architecture is concerned. The West Syrian Bishops tried to inculcate many West Syrian elements of church architecture along with the liturgical practices. To some extent their attempts were successful. The elements like the altar canopies and other ornate works in the sanctuary are examples for this.

Church architecture of Kerala is unique in many aspects. The age old Syrian heritage, culture and the beliefs and convictions about 'the Divine' is thoroughly envisaged in these spiritual edifices. Likewise are the elements of Theology which we observe in the architecture of churches in Kerala. The impact of signs, symbols and artefacts in church architecture, concerning the divine, on human mind is so great. These artefacts inside or outside of a church building ponders upon the scriptural truths, the faith and conviction of a believing community and this can indirectly influence the mind of a believer, positively, who participates in the worship at the same.

The present generation should be aware of the fact that there was a unique church architecture in Kerala. The St. Thomas Christians of Kerala should never lose their identity and trade-mark regarding church architecture, failing which is something that is highly disappointing. Utility is a factor that should be taken care of, but we should realize that there are certain deep roots, aspect wise and in theory, for building a place of worship; without realizing these, anyone can built great edifices in concrete, but these may not pertain to the criteria for a spiritual edifice. Even though, places of worship are built of materials of this world, they are consecrated as houses of the Almighty, in which dwells the glory of God. This should involve art and grandeur and theological symbols. Our forefathers realized this ultimate truth to a great extent and it reflected in church architecture of this land. All efforts should be made to preserve this great heritage. We need to search for, and go back to the roots of church architecture that bears the great testimony and faith of our fathers and mothers who toiled tirelessly to safeguard the faith, heritage and culture of our land.

Bibliography

Alex, Anupa Elizba. *Architecture: Space, Issues and Material,* Ahmedabad: CEPT University Press, 2013.

Binns, John. *An Introduction to the Christian Orthodox Churches.* Cambridge: Cambridge University Press, 2002.

Boner, Alice, Sadasiva Rath Sarma, Bettina Bäumer, *Vastusutra Upanishad: The Essence of Form in Sacred Art.* Delhi: Motilal Banarsidass Publishers, 1996.

Cherusseril, Mathew. *Kaduthuruthy Valiya Palli.* Kottayam: The Catholic Mission Press Training Centre, 1982.

Danielou, Jean. *Primitive Christian Symbols.* London: Spottiswoode Ballantyne and Co. Ltd, 1961.

Dillistone, F. W. *Traditional Symbols and the Contemporary World.* London: Epworth Press, 1968.

Doig, Allan. *Liturgy and Architecture.* London: Ashgate Publishing Limited, 2008.

Donnell, Kevin O'. *Postmodernism.* Oxford: Lion Publishing plc, 2003.

Edward, Sunil. *A Prelude to the Study of Indigenous, Pre-European, Church Architecture of Kerala,* Trivandrum: Chitkara University, 2014.

Hammond, Peter, ed. *Towards a Church Architecture.* London: The Architectural Press, 1962.

Jensen, Robin M. *The Substance if Things Seen.* Grand Rapids Michigan: Wm. B. Eerdmans Publishing Co, 2004.

Joseph, P. V. *Keraliya Vastuvidya Paramparyam.* Kozhikode: Mathrubhumi Books, 2012.

Kieckhefer, Richard. *Theology in Stone: Church Architecture from Byzantium to Berkeley.* Chennai: Oxford University Press, 2000.

Kurien, C.K. ed. *Kallooppara Valiya Palli- Sahashrabda Smaranika.* Thiruvalla: St. Mary's Church Publication, 2001.

Lowrie, Walter. *Art in the Early Church.* New York: Harper Torch Books/Harper & Row Publishers, 1965.

Malherbe, Abraham J. & Ferguson, Everett, tr., *The Life of Moses.* New York: Paulist Press, 1978.

Mar Athanasius, Thomas. *Nazrani Devalaya Vasthuvidya.* Kottayam: MOC Publications, 2007.

Mathew, Gervase. *Byzantine Aesthetics.* London: Jarrold and Sons Ltd. Norwich, 1963.

Mitchell, Margaret M. and Young, Frances M., ed., *The Cambridge History of Christianity,* Vol. 1. Cambridge: Cambridge University Press, 2006.

Mulamoottil, Abraham. *The Tent of the Pilgrim of Exile.* Thiruvalla: Peacepeopleplanet.org, 2016.

Mundadan, Mathias A. *The Arrival of Portuguese in India and The Thomas Christians* Bangalore: Dharmaram College, 1967.

Nair, A. Mohanakshan. *Vasthuvidya Christhava-Muslim Devalayangal.* Kottayam: D C Press (P) Ltd., 2009.

Ouspenky, Leonide. *Theology of the Icon.* New York: St. Vladimir's Seminary Press, 1978.

Panicker, Geevarghese. *The Church in the Syriac Tradition.* Kottayam: St. Ephrem Ecumenical Research Institute, 2010.

Perayil, Varghese. *Portuguese Heritage in Kerala: Some Dimensions.* Adoor: Department of History, St. Cyril's College, 2013.

Podippara, Placid J. *The Thomas Christians,* Bombay: St. Paul Publications, 1970.

Smith, Arthur E. *The Temple and Its Teaching,* Chicago: Moody Press, 1956.

Rajan, K. Mani. *Queen of Sacraments: A Treatise on the Liturgy of the Holy Mass Celebrated in the Syrian Orthodox Church.* Mulanthuruthy: Seminary Publications, 1994.

Schaff, Philip S. and Schaff, David S. *History of the Christian Church,* Vol. 5. New Delhi: Christian World Imprints, 2016.

Smalley, Stephen. *Building for Worship.* London: Hodder and Stoughton, 1967.

Steffler, Alva William. Symbols of the Christian Faith. Grand Rapids, Michigan: Wm. B. Eerdmans Publishing Co., 2002.

Thomas, Kurian K. *Thomayar Kovil- Thiruvithamcode Arachapally.* Kottayam: The Malankara Orthodox Church Publications, 2013.

Thomas, Meledath Kurian. *The Indian Way of Christianity.* Saarbruken, Deuschland: LAP LAMBERT Academic Publishing, 2012.

Vasudev, Gayathri Devi. *Vastu: Astrology and Architecture.* New Delhi: Motilal Banarsidass Publishers, 1995.

Vaux, Roland de. *Ancient Israel- Its Life and Institutions.* Great Britain: Darton, Longman & Todd Ltd, 1961.

Vazhuthanpally, Joseph. *The Biblical and Archaeological Foundations of the Mar Thoma Sliba.* Kottayam: Oriental Institute of Religious Studies India Publications, 1990.

Wunderlich, Robert E. *Worship and the Arts.* Missouri: Concordia Publishing House, 1966.

Web Sources

Chiotti, Roberto and Vosko, Richard S. "Worship Space Today", *Trends in Modern Church Architecture* (23 May, 2011): http://americamagazine.org/issue/777/ article/ worship-space-today.

McNamara, Denis. *"Built Form of Theology: The Natural Sympathies of Catholicismand Classicism"* Vol. 12, Sacred Architecture Journal (2016) http://www.sacredarchitecture. org/articles/built_form_of_theology.

Stetzer, Ed. Trends in Church Architecture, Part 1, http://www.christianitytoday.com/edstetzer/2016/july/trends-in-church-architecture-part-1.html.

Lew, Fr. Lawrence O.P. *The Theology and Metaphysics of the Gothic Cathedral - part 3* (09 May, 2009): http://www.sacredarchitecture.org/articles/a_decade_of_new_classicism_the_flowering_of_traditional_church_architecture.

Meistermann, B. Temple of Jerusalem. In The Catholic Encyclopedia. New York: Robert Appleton Company. Retrieved January 31, 2017 from New Advent: http://www.newadvent.org/cathen/14499a.htm.

Menachery, George. "Kerala Church Art and Architecture": European Influence on Church Art and Architecture of Kerala- Featured Paper, http://trijoindia.tripod.com/menacherypapers/id9.html (28 Jan. 2017). http://www.vaastu-shastra.com/vastu-vidya.html.

Rao, S. Sreenivasa. Temple Architecture-Devalaya Vastu, https://sreenivasaraos.com/2012/09/07/temple-architecture-devalaya-vastu-part-one-1-of-7.

Vaasthu Shastra- An Encyclopaedia on Vastu Shastra, http://www.vaastu-shastra.com/worship-room-tips.html.

http://www.bible-architecture.info/Jerusalem.htm (28 Jan. 2017).

http://www.crystalinks.com/solomonstemple. html (28 Jan. 2017).

https://www.fisheaters.com/symbols.html (02 Mar. 2017).

http://www.religionfacts.com/number-symbols (24 Feb. 2017).

Online Journal

Panjikaran S., Vedamuthu P., An Evaluation of Spatial Organization of the Church Architecture of Kerala during the Sixteenth to Seventeenth Centuries": Journal of The Institution of Engineers (India): Series A, May 2013, http://paperity.org/p/36563323/an-evaluation-of-spatial-organization-of-the-church-architecture-of-kerala-during-the (02 Feb. 2017).

Slick, Matt. *The Postmodern Mind* (08 Feb. 2000):

https://carm.org/emerging-church-postmodernism-The Emerging Church and Postmodernism.

Stroik, Duncan. "*The Roots of Modernist Church Architecture*", Adoremus Bulletin, Society for the Renewal of the Sacred Liturgy- Vol. III, No. 7 (October 1997): http://www.adoremus.org/1097-Stroik.html.

d. Valerie, Spanswick. *Medieval Churches: Sources and Forms,* https://www.khanacademy.org/humanities/medieval-world/latin-western-europe/romanesque1/a/medieval-churches-sources-and-forms.

Online Articles

Stephen Beale, *Ten Ways Noah's Ark Prefigured the Church- Catholic Exchange* (24 Mar. 2014) http://catholicexchange.com/ten-ways-noahs-ark-prefigured-church (24 Feb. 2017).

Joseph H. Peterson ed., *The Mystical Theology of Dionysius the Areopagite* (England: The Grade City Press Ltd., 2004), http://www.esotericarchives.com/oracle/ dionys1.htm (20 Feb. 2017).

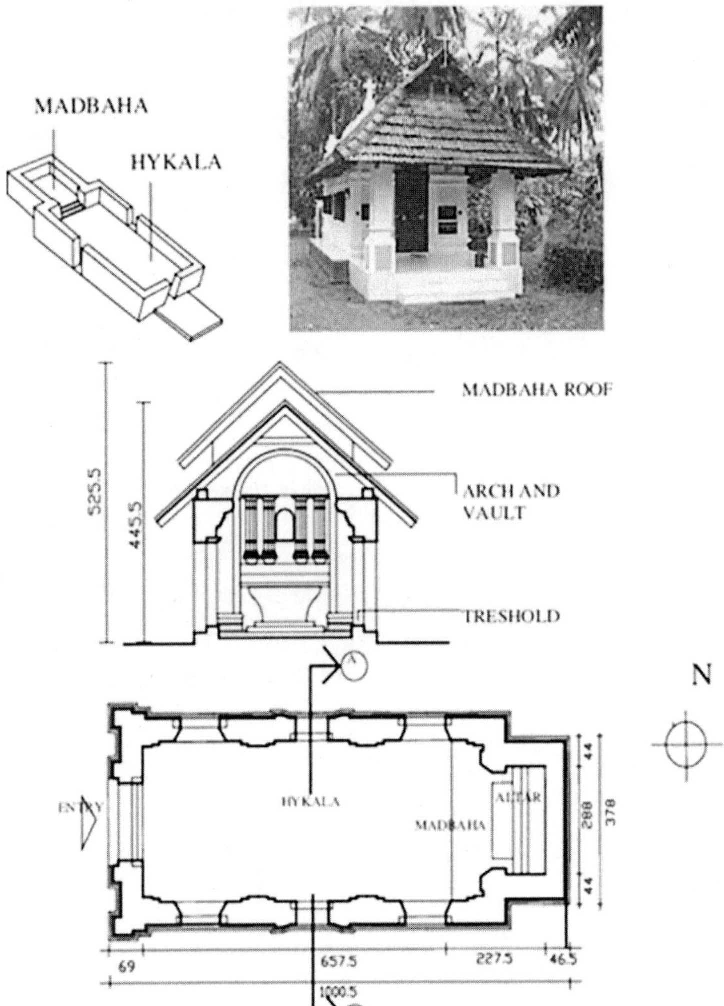

Diagrams showing the plan, elevation and cross sectional details of the ancient Syrian Church building.

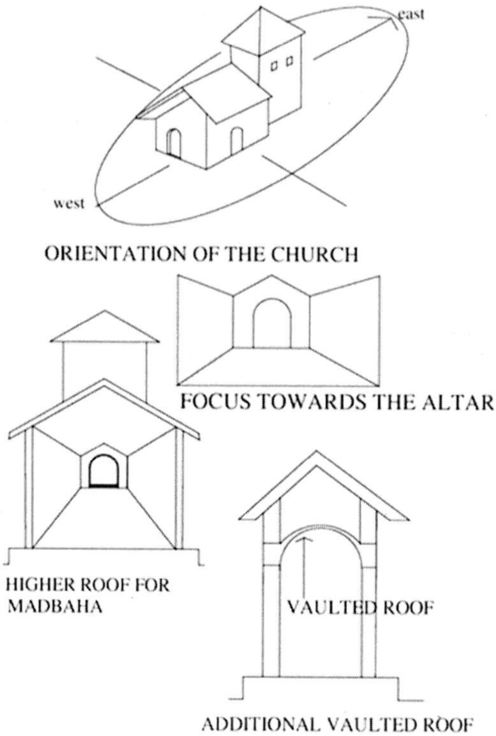

Figure showing the position and height of the sanctuary and nave of a traditional Syrian church.

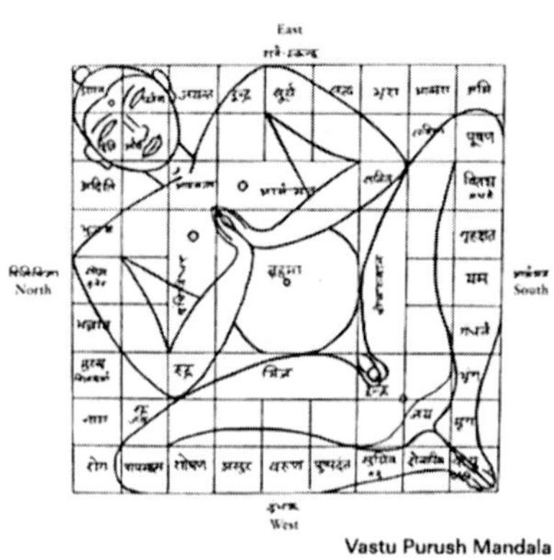

Figure showing Vastu Purusha Mandala.

Cross sectional view of the Temple of Jerusalem built by Solomon.

Dwarapalas- Makara, Kaduthuruthy.

Ancient Cross and Stone Inscription, Kaduthuruthy.

St. Mary's Orthodox Church, Kallooppara, Kerala (The ancient structure resembles very much the Hindu Temple). The *Poomukham* on the Northern side of the Church exhibits the traditional *Thachu shashtra* and *Vasthu vidhya.*

The Facade of the Kallooppara St. Mary's Church was put up after the advent of the Portuguese.

Picture showing the semi-circular vault of the Madbaha and the ornate canopies above the secondary altars at Kallooppara St. Mary's Church.

This ancient Church at Chengannoor (Old Syrian Church), has no windows (Window at the south west end is a late addition).

This huge stone cross at St. Mary's Knanaya Church, Kaduthuruthy depicts the ancient Nazrani Architectural Heritage.

The Eastern Wall below the roof of the Kaduthuruthy Church showing symbols of a hunter, deer and tiger.

This very old Baptismal Font made out of rock as found in Kaduthuruthy Church.

The Eastern Facade of the Kaduthuruthy Church exhibits Gothic Architecture and Bas-relief of Christian Signs and Symbols.

The ornate wooden canopy (Small Kudish-Kudishin) found
in the sanctuary of St. Thomas Orthodox Church Karthikapally.

The West side Facade of Karthikapally St. Thomas Church
(This was the pattern of facade before the Portuguese influence.

The intricately adorned Kudish-Kudishin (Altar canopy) at the
Sanctuary and secondary altars of Old Seminary Chapel, Kottayam.

The South-West view of the Thiruvithamcode St. Mary's Orthodox Church (One of the oldest existing Church structures in the world-resembles a Hindu Temple).

Another view of the Church (The Architecture in Rock pertains to the local temple architecture with Christian Symbolic elements richly adorns the structure).

The intricate carvings in stone (Depictions of Eucharistic bread, chalice, angels and other floral designs-dates back to the early centuries, 6th-7th century C.E).

Common architectural elements in Churches and Temples

Gabled Roof (Church)

Gabled Roof (Temple)

Porch adjoining the nave

Temple Church

Gabled Roof (Temple)

Circular Gabled Roof

Church

Temple

Facade

Church

Temple

Sanctuary

Church

Temple

Rock cut Pillars

Church

Temple

Sanctum Sanctorum of a Hindu Temple

Thiruvithamcode St. Mary's Orthodox Church- Built
by Apostle St. Thomas: One of the Oldest Existing Church Structure
(6th Century C. E).